Sigmund Freud

Sigmund Freud
PIONEER OF THE MIND

by Catherine Reef

CLARION BOOKS ◉ NEW YORK

Conducting the research for this book gave me the opportunity to work with archivists in Austria, France, Great Britain, and Greece. I thank the following individuals for their courtesy and assistance: Mathieu Michel, Compagnie des Wagons-Lits, Paris; Dr. Hans R. Goette, German Archaeological Institute, Athens; Rita Apsan, Freud Museum, London; Simon Conti, Mary Evans Picture Library, London; Brigitte Maurer, Institute for the History of Medicine, Vienna; Helmut Selzer, Vienna Museum of History; and Dr. Elisabeth Klamper, Archive of the Austrian Resistance, Vienna.

Excerpts from *The Letters of Sigmund Freud*, copyright © 1960 by Sigmund Freud Copyrights Ltd., copyright renewed, are reprinted by permission of Basic Books, a member of Perseus Books, L.L.C. For additional rights/territory, contact Sigmund Freud Copyrights Ltd., 10 Brook Street, Wivenhoe, Colchester CO790DS, England.

PICTURE CREDITS

Archives Compagnie des Wagons-Lits © Wagons-Lits Diffusion 2000, Paris, France: viii · Library of Congress: 2, 11, 13, 14, 19, 23, 33, 38, 46, 55, 58, 59, 60, 69, 71, 72, 73, 75, 84, 85, 89, 91, 94, 97, 103, 106, 118, 126, 131, 134 Deutsches Archaeologisches Institut, Athens, neg. MYK 63: 3 · Freud Museum, London: 4, 5, 7, 10, 52, 56, 61, 86, 99, 115, 117, 119, 128, 130 Mary Evans/Sigmund Freud Copyrights: 8, 16, 24, 27, 48, 50, 58, 121, 122· National Library of Medicine: 29, 37, 40, 44, 45, 47, 100 · Institut für Geschichte der Medizin der Universität Wien: 31, 36, 42 · Historisches Museum der Stadt Wien: 35 · John Reef: 64, 92 · *The Prophets Elijah, Moses, Joshua,* a mural by John Singer Sargent. Photograph from the collection of the Library of Congress: 78 · National Archives: 110, 125 · Stiftung Dokumentationsarchiv des Österreichischen Widerstandes: 123

Clarion Books · a Houghton Mifflin Company imprint · 215 Park Avenue South, New York, NY 10003 · Copyright © 2001 by Catherine Reef · Book design by Trish Parcell. · The text was set in 11-point New Aster. · All rights reserved. · For information about permission to reproduce selections from this book, write to Permissions, Houghton Mifflin Company, 215 Park Avenue South, New York, NY 10003. · www.houghtonmifflinbooks.com · Printed in the U.S.A.

Library of Congress Cataloging-in-Publication Data · Reef, Catherine. · Sigmund Freud : pioneer of the mind / by Catherine Reef. · p. cm. · Includes bibliographical references. · ISBN 0-618-01762-3 · 1. Freud, Sigmund, 1856–1939–Juvenile literature. 2. Psychoanalysts—Austria—Biography—Juvenile literature. 3. Psychoanalysis—Juvenile literature. [1. Freud, Sigmund, 1856–1939. 2. Psychoanalysts. 3. Psychoanalysis.] · BF109.F74 R44 2001 · 150.19'52'092—dc21 · [B] · 00-043008 ·

RO 10 9 8 7 6 5 4 3 2 1

For my mother

Contents

"Act as though . . . you were a traveller
sitting next to the window
of a railway carriage . . ."

CHAPTER ONE

Wrestling Demons

"Say whatever goes through your mind." The doctor told his patient, a woman of eighteen, not to worry about making sense. He asked her to speak her thoughts as they occurred to her, one right after another. "Act as though, for instance, you were a traveller sitting next to the window of a railway carriage," he said, "and describing to someone inside the carriage the changing views which you see outside."

With those words, Sigmund Freud, M.D., of Vienna, Austria, led his patient on a psychological journey. Together they were going to explore the innermost workings of her mind.

The young woman lying on the couch had been to many doctors, but none of them had examined her in this way. The other doctors had labeled her symptoms—the coughing spells, the blackouts, the suicide threat—hysteria. And hysteria, they believed, was a physical ailment. They had prescribed soothing baths and electric shocks, the regimen most often used to treat

One of Sigmund Freud's children took this photograph of him in the early twentieth century.

hysteria in Europe and America in 1900. But those methods had brought no relief.

The patient looked around. The room seemed more like a museum than a doctor's office. Carved figures from Greece, Egypt, and other ancient civilizations crowded the mantelpiece. Paintings and prints covered the walls. The room was weighed down with the heavy, dark furniture and patterned rugs that were stylish in the last decades of the nineteenth century. This was the consulting room of Dr. Freud.

Freud offered a new approach to hysteria. He was convinced that symptoms like the ones this woman displayed did not result from a physical problem. He was sure that their cause lay deep within the mind.

Dressed neatly in a well-pressed suit, his hair and beard carefully trimmed, Freud sat behind the couch, out of the woman's view. He puffed on a cigar, and his dark eyes focused on a scene outside the window. He was listening to what his patient said, to the connections she made between the present and the past, among her dreams, her wishes, and her fears.

Freud often felt like the archaeologists finding priceless relics in ruined, ancient cities such as Troy. An archaeologist, he said, sees beyond the obvious. To him or her, crumbling walls are "the ramparts of a palace or a treasure house." Inscriptions in weathered stone "reveal an alphabet and a language, and when they have been deciphered and translated, yield undreamed-of information about the events of the remote past." Like an archaeologist of the mind, Freud waited for his patient's words to reveal their hidden messages: long-lost memories and unconscious desires.

Sigmund Freud explored the human mind more thoroughly than anyone who had come before him. He pioneered a new method for diagnosing and treating mental illness, a method he called psychoanalysis. He simply talked to his patients, and, more important, he listened.

Freud found that some events and impulses were too frightening or painful for his patients to acknowledge. Their minds locked away this disturbing material in a region he called the unconscious. According to Freud, such thoughts are never forgotten, even though they are kept out of the conscious, waking mind. Like a pebble lodged inside a person's shoe, they make their presence known. They might erupt as physical ailments that have no apparent cause, or as psychological symptoms, such as abnormal fears or obsessions. Freud said that unconscious memories and impulses govern human behavior to a greater degree than most people suspected. His goal in psychoanalysis was to make the unconscious known.

Over a period of months or even years, Freud helped his patients bring unconscious material to the surface, one buried memory at a time. This was hard work. It seemed to him that part of the patient's conscious mind resisted facing up to painful truths. "One gets the impression of a demon striving not to come to the light of day," he wrote to a friend.

According to the teachings of psychoanalysis, once people become aware of their unconscious thoughts, they can start to

Like many Europeans of his time, Freud was captivated by the discoveries of German archaeologist Heinrich Schliemann. Schliemann excavated the ancient cities of Troy and Mycenae in the 1870s. In this photograph, nineteenth-century tourists pose on and around the Lion Gate that marks the entrance to Mycenae, near the modern Greek town of Mikinai.

Freud's couch, one of the most famous pieces of furniture in the world, is housed today at the Freud Museum in London. Hundreds of patients reclined on this couch to analyze their thoughts and emotions with Dr. Freud as a guide.

understand them. Freud's patients submitted to psychoanalysis for the self-knowledge and freedom from symptoms that they hoped to achieve.

By the turn of the twentieth century, psychoanalysis was gaining some attention. Several young physicians were excited by Freud's ideas and eager to try them out. Yet the medical establishment on the whole shunned Freud. One prominent doctor dismissed psychoanalysis as a "scientific fairy tale." Another denounced Freud on the basis of his heritage, calling psychoanalysis a "Jewish swindle." Others had even harsher criticism. "This is not a topic for discussion at a scientific meeting," one researcher cried, "it is a matter for the police."

It was not the role of the unconscious that bothered the stiff-necked doctors of that era, but Freud's focus on sexuality. Freud had concluded that the unconscious memories and urges governing people's behavior are often sexual in nature. More shocking was the notion that erotic feelings are not limited to adulthood. Freud said that sexuality is part of human life from infancy.

Throughout his life, Freud responded to criticism by carrying out his work and publishing more results. "What is new has always aroused bewilderment and resistance," he stated. In his later writings, he applied his insight to the riddle of dreams and described the workings of the healthy human mind.

The force of Freud's ideas overpowered many of the arguments against them, at least for a while. By the time he was an old man, Freud had become one of the most famous people in the world. He is now considered one of the most influential figures of the twentieth century. Freudian psychology has changed the way people do many things, from creating literature and art to bringing up their children.

Japanese students of psychoanalysis, photographed in 1930.

But despite their vast influence, Freud's teachings are under renewed attack. For instance, Freud's focus on sexuality still raises hackles. Many people perceive it to be a reaction to his straitlaced times. Also, much of the modern criticism concerns his research methods, which fall short of the rigorous standards that investigators follow today. Critics point out that Freud did most of his work within a narrow segment of the population—upper-

middle-class European women with psychological problems. It is a stretch, they say, to apply findings based on this work to the entire human race.

Some of the strongest recent criticism comes from feminist thinkers. They assert that Freud's analyses of female patients, including the troubled eighteen-year-old who lay on his couch in 1900, were biased and possibly even harmful. One such critic, Kate Millett, has observed that the women of Freud's day were expected to play a protected, passive role in society. Capable women who saw men freely pursue artistic or intellectual interests suffered psychological pain. Millett has argued that Freud did all women a grievous wrong when he overlooked the consequences of social inequality.

Advances in pharmacology have led to further criticism. Psychiatrists can now treat or control some mental health problems with drugs, and many are questioning the value of psychoanalysis. They call it a costly, time-consuming therapy with an uncertain outcome. One doctor has written, "I was used to seeing patients' personalities change slowly, through painfully acquired insight and practice in the world. But recently I have seen personalities altered almost instantly, by medication."

Today's growing reliance on medication would not surprise Sigmund Freud. He once said, "Let the biologists go as far as they can and let us go as far as we can—one day the two will meet." He viewed his work as a beginning and admitted that his findings had yet to be firmly established. He envied physicists and mathematicians who could present clear proof of the results of their work.

For reasons that are unclear, people no longer respond to mental distress with the set of symptoms that the doctors of

Freud's era labeled hysteria. Psychiatrists now use the term "conversion symptom" when referring to a psychological problem that presents itself as a physical ailment. The number of people with conversion reactions is unknown, but the disorder occurs most often in women and young adults. Those who are afflicted are likely to have had a serious illness in the past or to be dealing with grief or other psychological stress.

Medical terms have changed, but the debate goes on: Was Freud right or wrong? At the same time, his ideas are so widespread that they color our view of human conduct in ways that may not be apparent. It is impossible to understand psychology at the start of the twenty-first century without some knowledge of Freud.

In June 1938, Sigmund Freud stepped off a boat and onto the southern coast of England. Eighty-two years old and ravaged by cancer, he had been forced to flee his beloved Vienna following Nazi Germany's annexation of Austria. Freud knew he had only a short time to live, but he planned to press ahead with his work—to analyze patients and to write. He had learned to live with persecution and pain. As he had noted more than three decades earlier, "No one who, like me, conjures up the most evil of those half-tamed demons that inhabit the human breast, and seeks to wrestle with them, can expect to come through the struggle unscathed."

Upon his arrival in London, Freud was greeted by his oldest daughter, Mathilde Hollitscher, who stands to his right. Freud's daughter-in-law, Lucie Freud, and a British colleague, Ernest Jones, welcomed him as well.

"If a man has been his mother's
undisputed darling . . . "

CHAPTER TWO

Favorite Son

The Freuds of Kaiser Josefstrasse (Kaiser Josef Street), Vienna, often repeated their favorite stories when they gathered at the table. With her husband and large brood listening, Amalia Freud liked to relive a visit she had made to a pastry shop years earlier.

Amalia had been waiting in the busy shop to make a purchase, holding her oldest child, Sigmund, in her arms. An aged woman approached, drawn by the toddler's shining black hair and intelligent gaze. Like the craggy soothsayer in a fairy tale, the woman proclaimed that the child would be a great man someday.

Sigmund Freud always listened to his mother's story with smiling good humor, but he put little stock in it. Omens and blind belief held no appeal for him. He wanted a full explanation for everything. "Such prophecies must be made very frequently," he reasoned. "There are so many happy and expectant mothers and so many old peasant women, and other old women who . . . turn their eyes toward the future."

Sigmund Freud, age 16, with his mother.

Freud's birthplace, the town of Freiberg.

But for Amalia Freud, the prediction confirmed what she knew to be true. She doted on her Sigi, who was so handsome and quick to learn. Throughout his childhood and youth, she would have nothing but the best for him, even demanding sacrifices from other family members. A grown-up Freud traced his conquering spirit and professional achievement to Amalia's love and support. He wrote, "If a man has been his mother's undisputed darling he retains throughout life the triumphant feeling, the confidence in success, which not seldom brings actual success along with it."

In 1855, when pretty, fun-loving Amalia Nathansohn was twenty years old, she married a man nearly twice her age. Jacob Freud was a wool merchant, a widower, and a grandfather who had a kind and hopeful nature. The couple made their home on the second floor of a house in the Moravian town of Freiberg (now Příbor, Czech Republic), sharing the space with a locksmith and his family. Sigmund was born there on May 6, 1856.

As a young child in Freiberg, Sigmund played rough-and-tumble games with his nephew John. The son of Freud's half-brother Emanuel, John was a year older than his uncle Sigi. The boys had a girl to tease when John's sister Pauline grew old enough to join their games.

Sigi was not his mother's only child for long. His birth was soon followed by that of a brother. Baby Julius turned out to be sickly, though, and he died at eight months of age. A sister arrived on the last day of 1858. Amalia and Jacob breathed a sigh of relief when they saw that Anna was plump and sturdy.

The Freuds hired a nanny to look after the children. Freud remembered her as "that prehistoric old woman," ugly and severe. Nanny was Czech and a Catholic, like most of Freiberg's five thousand people, and she took the little Jewish boy to Mass without his parents' knowledge. The woman was less than honest in other ways, too. When Jacob and Amalia discovered her stealing toys and money from their home, they promptly had her arrested and hauled off to jail.

Sigi asked where Nanny was, and his half-brother Philipp explained that she had been locked up. Philipp's response led to an occurrence that was recalled many times when the family shared stories: One day when Amalia went to town, Sigi was upset because he could not find her anywhere. Crying, he begged Philipp to unlock a large chest that was kept in the house and let his mother out.

In this childhood portrait, Freud's eyes already wear the penetrating expression that was typical of his adult years.

Life in Freiberg was eventful, but Jacob and his grown sons were forced to admit that they had no future there. For twenty years, the textile industry had been dying out in European villages. Machines could work faster and more cheaply than country people, and factories were going up in cities and large towns, drawing work away from places like Freiberg. The recently completed Northern Railway bypassed the town altogether.

The political situation also caused concern. Moravia belonged to the Austrian Empire, a powerful nation stretching from Switzerland to Russia. In building its empire, Austria had conquered the homelands of several ethnic groups. The Slavs, Hungarians, Croats, Czechs, and other non-Austrian peoples of the empire resented their iron-fisted rulers, the royal Habsburg family. Each group valued its own language and traditions, and longed for independence.

People of Austrian descent were angry with their leaders as well. They wanted the personal liberty that had been granted to citizens in other countries, such as the United States and France. In March 1848, eight years before Freud was born, students and civic groups in the capital city, Vienna, demanded freedom of speech and freedom of the press. They called for a constitution and a bill of rights. When the government ignored their petitions, the Viennese rioted.

Acting swiftly, Archduke Albrecht, commanding general of the National Guard, ordered his men to attack the protesters. The several citizens who died in the clash that followed were remembered as the "Fallen Ones of March." Their deaths gave courage to Austrian workers, who burned factories in outrage. Throughout the empire, in Budapest, Prague, and other cities, ethnic peoples rose in revolt against the imperial regime.

Fires light up the sky over Vienna during the uprising of 1848.

The army snuffed out the uprisings in a matter of months. Emperor Ferdinand I stepped down, and his eighteen-year-old nephew, Franz Josef, assumed the throne. The new leader proved to be a young tyrant who imposed brutal repression.

Old resentments festered in Freiberg and elsewhere. Many Czech textile workers turned against the Jewish merchants who lived among them, blaming the Jews for their woes. They pointed out that the Jews spoke German, just like the Habsburgs.

The new railroads made it easy for country people to pick up and move to the city. In 1860, Jacob and Amalia Freud took their small children to Vienna. Philipp, Emanuel, and Emanuel's family followed a different course and sailed to England. Sigmund's half-brothers hoped to find work in the city of Manchester, known for its textile mills.

Vienna was a glorious place, one of the liveliest cities in

Europe. It was famous for its majestic architecture, rolling park-land, and stylish homes. Sitting beside the Danube River and surrounded on three sides by woods, Vienna offered scenic views in every direction. The city was a center of culture and learning. People traveled for miles to hear a concert there, or to consult a distinguished doctor.

Vienna was also the fastest-growing major city in Europe. The population, which was 440,000 in 1840, would pass two million in 1910. Day after day, uprooted small-town people embarking on a new life spilled out of trains. They came from every corner of the empire—from Hungary, Croatia, Galicia, Bohemia, and Moravia. Many of the newcomers were Jews. At the time of Sigmund's

Vienna, Austria, Freud's home for most of his life, as it appeared in the late nineteenth century.

birth, Jews accounted for one percent of the population of Vienna. By the turn of the twentieth century, one in ten Viennese would be Jewish.

There was not enough room for so many people. If they were lucky, a newly arrived family found a place to live in Vienna. Those less fortunate sought shelter in shanties and abandoned railroad cars on the outskirts of the city.

The Freuds were among the lucky ones, settling in a tiny apartment in a Jewish neighborhood. There, the family grew rapidly. Over the next few years, Sigi and Anna welcomed a string of new sisters: Rosa, Marie, Adolfine, and Pauline. The youngest child, Alexander, was born in 1866. Sigi referred to himself and his brother as a pair of bookends—two boys standing at either end of a line of girls.

Money was tight in the Freud household, because Jacob had trouble finding a steady job. He took whatever work he could find, never letting the hard times get him down. Freud called his father an optimist, a person "always expecting something to turn up." Wanting his children to have a better life than his own, Jacob stressed the value of an education. He and Amalia gave Sigi lessons as soon as the boy could learn. When he was old enough, they sent him to school.

School was a stern place in nineteenth-century Vienna. The teacher sat on a high platform, and the pupils called him Professor. He seldom smiled and rarely explained anything. All day long, he listened while the class recited lessons from memory. He also drilled the children, asking one question after another to be sure that they had done their homework.

Sigmund adapted quickly to the routine of school and was one of the best students in his class. He spent many hours at his desk at home, poring over books, recording his dreams in a note-book, and looking out the window at the street. He was curious about everything. He read the Bible when he was seven and tack-led Shakespeare's plays at eight. He had no patience for his text-books, with the watered-down information they offered. Yearning for a deeper understanding of the world, he turned to scholarly books and technical manuals.

Sigmund Freud was about eight years old when he posed for this portrait with his father.

The other Freud children grew up in Sigi's shadow. They watched him win prizes for academic success, and they heard their mother brag about his early accomplishments so many times that they came to know the stories by heart.

And when Sigi was studying, they were not to make a sound. One day, he complained that Anna's piano practicing disturbed his concentration. (Freud disliked music throughout his life.) She must stop taking music lessons, he insisted, and the piano had to go. The family promptly obeyed him, and Anna stifled her dreams of becoming a musician.

Later on, when Sigi was seventeen, he took it upon himself to choose books for Anna to read. He told her that, in his opinion, novels by the French authors Honoré de Balzac and Alexandre Dumas were not suitable for a girl of fifteen. Of course, that made Anna want to read the forbidden books more than ever, so she hid them in her underwear drawer, where Sigi would never find them.

It is no wonder that as a child Freud liked to read about military leaders, men who were always barking out orders. His favorite was Hannibal, the illustrious general from the ancient city of Carthage. In the third century B.C., Hannibal led forty thousand soldiers and many horses and elephants over the Alps in an attempt to attack Rome, Carthage's bitter rival. Historians call Hannibal's march one of the greatest military feats of all time. The army made it over the Alps in fifteen days, surviving blizzards, landslides, and battles with the mountain people. Hannibal captured several smaller Roman cities, but his enemies kept him out of Rome itself. After more wars and numerous battles, the Romans eventually defeated Hannibal and forced him to flee Carthage.

Sigi also read about the French emperor Napoleon, another great military commander. He learned the name of every marshal serving under Napoleon, and he labeled his toy soldiers with their names in order to reenact battles.

War became real for Freud when he was ten years old and Austria fought against neighboring Prussia. Jacob Freud took his son to the railroad station to watch as wounded soldiers arrived in Vienna. The bleeding and bandaged young men cried out in pain as they were lifted into the hay carts that would carry them to a hospital. Anna now saw her brother's compassionate side. "Sigi was greatly impressed by the plight of the wounded," she recalled many years later. Anna and the other schoolgirls were making *Charpie*, soft pads of linen used to cleanse battlefield wounds. "He begged my mother to let him have all her old linen so that from it he could make 'Charpie,'" Anna said of her older brother. Wanting to help the soldiers, Sigi organized *Charpie* groups among the boys in his school.

In 1867, Austria granted the Hungarian people their independence. The Austrian Empire and Hungary became two nations, each with its own constitution, parliament, and courts. But they were not entirely separate. They flew the same flag and were ruled by the same man, Franz Josef, who was called emperor in Austria and king in Hungary. The two countries were known as the Dual Monarchy or Austria-Hungary. In 1871, Prussia united with other German states to form the nation of Germany.

Although scenes of battle inspired his imagination, Freud had no plans to be a soldier himself. He had a different ambition, formed one evening when he was eleven and the family was dining in a lively café. A poet strolled among the tables, pausing to think up a rhyme for anyone who tossed him a coin. When he reached the Freuds' table, he composed a few verses about Sigmund. This studious boy would grow up to be a government minister, the poet announced. The idea of telling the emperor what to do appealed to bossy Sigi Freud. He decided, then and there, to make the poet's words come true. He made up his mind to study law and become an important person in government.

He discussed the future in some of the long, serious talks he had with his father. They often conversed while walking along the streets of Vienna. One day, the topic of anti-Semitism came up. Jacob told his son about a time when a man had knocked his hat off and snarled, "Jew, get off the pavement!"

Sigmund asked, "And what did you do?" He wanted to hear every detail about how his father had fought back against the bully. But Jacob Freud only shrugged. "I went into the street and picked up the cap," he said.

His father's meekness disappointed Sigi. Jews were wrong to give in to taunting and hatred, the boy believed. He vowed that as a Jew in Vienna, he would always stand up for his rights.

Sigi felt lucky to count his father among his friends. Another close friend was Eduard Silberstein, a boy he had met in school. "We became friends at a time when one doesn't look upon friendship as a sport or an asset, but when one needs a friend with whom to share things. We used to be together literally every hour of the day that was not spent on the school bench," Freud wrote as an adult. If Sigi was not at Eduard's home, then Eduard was at his. "We shared our frugal suppers and were never bored in each other's company," Freud said.

Franz Josef, ruler of the Austrian Empire from 1848 until 1916.

The boys created a secret society with themselves as its only members. They learned some Spanish together, and they chose new names from the pages of *Don Quixote,* the early-seventeenth-century Spanish novel by Miguel de Cervantes. Foreign languages were a snap for Sigmund. He learned English, French, Latin, and Greek in school, and he studied Hebrew in after-school religion classes. He picked up Italian and Spanish on his own.

In the summer of 1872, when he was sixteen, Freud rode a train to Freiberg to visit some family friends. The Flüsses had five children, three boys and two girls. He promptly fell in love with fifteen-year-old Gisela Flüss, a tan, healthy girl with long black hair. He thought about Gisela in her bright yellow dress even as he hiked in the wooded foothills of the Carpathian Mountains or revisited the scenes of his early childhood. He rehearsed what he was going to say to her, but whenever they met he felt too nervous to speak. Gisela made things worse by playing jokes on him.

Sigi went home at the end of his vacation regretting that he had not confessed his love. But once school started, he was too busy for romance. This was his final year at the Sperlgymnasium, his secondary school. He had to buckle down and prepare for the *Matura,* which was the big final exam before graduation. In a year he would be starting university.

Jacob Freud encouraged his son's interest in a political career by hanging portraits of Jewish members of government in the Freud home. Sigmund, however, was changing his mind about the future. He was excited by the ideas of Charles Darwin, the English scientist who had put forth the theory of evolution. In 1859, Darwin's book *On the Origin of Species* had shaken up the scientific world by describing a natural order in which new plant and animal species evolved from earlier ones. All living things, including human beings, were the products of evolution, according to Darwin.

This notion shocked many religious people. They pointed to passages in the Bible as proof that God had created all animal species just as they now appeared, unchangeable for all time. And the idea that people were merely animals was scandalous. Yet to Freud and others, Darwin's theory held the promise that science, and not religion, would answer the great questions that perplexed humankind.

Early in 1873, Sigmund heard Carl Brühl, a highly respected professor, give a lecture in Vienna. Brühl read from an essay titled "Nature," wrongly attributed to Johann Wolfgang von Goethe, a great German writer who died in 1832. "'Nature! We are surrounded and embraced by her: powerless to separate ourselves from her, and powerless to penetrate beyond her,'" Professor Brühl read. "'She is ever shaping new forms: what is, has never yet been; what has been, comes not again. Everything is new, and yet nought but the old.'"

Freud came home inspired. He wrote excitedly to Gisela's brother, Emil Flüss, "I shall gain insight into the age-old dossiers of Nature, perhaps even eavesdrop on her eternal processes, and share my findings with anyone who wants to learn." He was going to be a scientist.

The future belonged to science—that was the message of the World Exhibition, which opened in Vienna on May 1, 1873. In a huge building with a central domed rotunda that was 312 feet across, fifty thousand exhibitors showcased the products of Austrian technology for the entire world to see. Everyone agreed that the grand circular room was a sight to behold. Some looked on it as the "eighth wonder of the world," while others laughed and called it "an enormous cake." There was no disputing the fact that this exhibition was bigger than any other industrial display that Europe had ever seen. It was five times larger than the Paris Expo of 1867, the Viennese boasted.

One of the seven million people who toured the World Exhibition was Sigi Freud. "Interesting," he wrote to Emil Flüss, "but it didn't bowl me over." The seventeen-year-old Freud felt too smart to be impressed by such a gaudy show. "On the whole it is a display for the aesthetic, precious, and superficial world, which also for the most part visits it," his letter continued. Yet he planned to attend the exhibition every day in summer, once he was done with the *Matura* and life was free and easy. "One can also be gloriously alone there in all that crowd" was his excuse.

Amalia Freud's heart filled with pride when her "golden Sigi" passed the *Matura* with high marks. Jacob promised his son a trip to England as a reward for so much hard work.

Sigmund looked forward to the trip in two years, and to entering the University of Vienna in the fall, even though the summer turned out to be less carefree than he had hoped. An outbreak of cholera in the city claimed two thousand lives. Then the Vienna and Berlin stock markets crashed. Insurance companies, banks, and other enterprises closed in the months that followed. The change was dramatic and frightening. Seventy-two banks were doing business in Vienna at the time of the crash, but only fourteen would be operating five years later.

Most of the city's banks had been founded by Jewish businessmen. Now, just as in Freiberg when Sigmund was small, the Jews served as scapegoats during tough times. A rumor spread through Vienna that Jews were behind the economic crisis, that they were somehow profiting from the misfortune of their neigh-

Visitors relax beside the Schwanenbassin, or swan pool, near the rotunda of the Vienna World Exhibition.

bors. Newspapers printed anti-Semitic cartoons. One showed a group of Jews marching under a banner that read "Masters over the World."

Freud understood that he was wise to pursue science instead of law. A young Jew would never succeed in government in such a climate of hatred.

The World Exhibition of 1873 included a replica of a rural American school.

"I was expected to feel myself inferior and an alien because I was a Jew."

CHAPTER THREE

Becoming a Doctor

The professors at the University of Vienna never taught a more energetic student than Sigmund Freud. He enrolled in the classes required for a medical degree and in many others that captured his interest. Along with anatomy and physiology, he studied philosophy, physics, botany, chemistry, zoology, mineralogy, and logic. He took a course called "Biology and Darwinism," and another called "The Physiology of Voice and Speech."

Freud loved learning the principles of science and the history of ideas. But university taught him lessons that he had not bargained for, as well. "I found that I was expected to feel myself inferior and an alien because I was a Jew," he wrote.

Vienna's recent growth had changed the university population. The Jews who had come to the city were people who valued learning. They were drawn to the school, both to teach and to study. By the late nineteenth century, nearly one-third of the medical school's professors were Jewish. Many Jews taught in

The University of Vienna at the time Freud studied there.

other divisions of the university, and the number of Jewish students was growing.

Christian faculty members, alarmed at this trend, argued against hiring more Jewish teachers, or as they put it, "further Judaicizing" the school. The university fraternities denied membership to Jewish students, so Freud was barred from the parties and dueling matches that fraternity men enjoyed. (All of Freud's fellow students were men. Although women were permitted to enroll in universities throughout Europe, few had done so by 1873, and none had entered the University of Vienna.)

If Sigmund Freud still intended to stand up to anti-Semitism, now was not the time. "I put up, without much regret, with my non-acceptance into the community," he noted, "for it seemed to me that in spite of this exclusion an active fellow-worker could not fail to find some nook or cranny in the framework of humanity."

Indeed, Freud soon found a niche for himself in the laboratory. He met no prejudice while looking through the lens of a microscope. Working alongside his professors in their labs, he was doing actual hands-on science, and he loved it. The laboratory was where real learning took place, where scientists added to humanity's great body of knowledge.

Sigmund thought about his future in science during the summer of 1875, when he visited Manchester. He liked everything about England, including the foggy, rainy climate. He easily imagined making his home there. "Perhaps, dear friend," he wrote to his boyhood companion, Eduard Silberstein, "after the conclusion of my studies a favorable wind may blow me to England for my practical work." That work, he dreamed, might benefit humankind. One day it might "restrict some of the evils which befall our bodies or . . . remove them from the world."

Freud was as impressed with his half-brothers and their families as he was with their adopted country. His brothers were now respected merchants. Emanuel sold cloth, while Philipp was a jeweler. Sigmund's nephew John, his playmate from Freiberg, had grown into "an Englishman in every sense with a knowledge of languages and technical matters greater than that of most business people," Freud wrote to Silberstein.

The English Freuds found much to praise about their guest as well. "You have given us great pleasure by sending us Sigmund," Emanuel stated in a letter to Vienna. "He is a splendid specimen of a fine human being."

The Freud family in 1876. Standing, left to right, are Pauline, Anna, Sigmund, Emanuel (on a visit to Vienna), Rosa, Marie, and a cousin, Simon Nathansohn. Adolfine, Amalia, Alexander, and Jacob occupy the chairs. The identities of the other two children—the girl in white and the boy sitting on the floor—are unknown.

Sigmund returned home itching to travel again. In his third year of study, his zoology professor secured funds to send him to the Zoological Experimentation Station at Trieste. (This prosperous Italian port was then under Austrian rule.) There, Freud studied the anatomy of eels. Scientists at that time had yet to examine an adult male eel, and they were curious to do so. Freud dissected four hundred eels to look at their reproductive organs, but he found no males. He wondered whether eels develop male sexual organs at a more advanced stage in their life cycle, a hypothesis later proved correct.

Freud had gone to Trieste eager to make an important discovery and returned to Vienna thinking he had failed. The mysteries of eel reproduction would not be solved until the twentieth century, when scientists found the eels' spawning beds in the Sargasso Sea.

Freud worked next in the physiology laboratory of Professor Ernst Brücke, a man with a gruff manner and steely eyes. Sigmund never forgot the morning when he arrived late at the laboratory and found Professor Brücke waiting for him at the door. "What he said to me was brief and to the point," Freud recalled. "But it was not what he said that mattered. What overwhelmed me was the terrible gaze of his blue eyes, before which I melted away." Brücke was a tough taskmaster, yet if he saw a student striving to learn, he went out of his way to offer help. He was a brilliant scientist, cautious and thorough, and he soon earned Freud's loyalty.

Brücke was investigating the minute structures in nerve cells. In the 1870s, physiologists were carrying on a hot debate: Were the nervous systems of lower animals—of worms, mollusks, and the like—similar in structure to the nervous systems of mammals, or were they different? It was a question that tested people's core beliefs. The answer could refute Darwin's theory or bolster it. If Brücke proved that the human nervous system was like that of the crayfish, his findings would support the notion that human beings were a product of evolution.

Brücke's institute hardly looked like the outstanding research center that it was. Housed in the ground floor and basement rooms of an old gun factory, it was damp, dark, and foul-smelling. The rooms lacked running water and natural gas for lighting.

In that gloomy environment, Freud looked at nerve cells from the larvae of lampreys, which are primitive fish. He found those cells to be similar in structure to spinal ganglia, cells in higher animals from which long nerve fibers radiate. His was one of many small discoveries that supported Darwin's ideas.

Freud made another contribution to science when he devised a method for staining tissue samples. In order to see tiny structures within cells clearly through a microscope, researchers stain their samples with chemicals. Freud found that gold chloride, a yellow compound, was an effective stain for nerve cells.

When he finished his day's work, Sigmund hurried home to bone up for his classes. The Freuds were now living in a larger apartment, on Kaiser Josefstrasse. It had three bedrooms, a dining room, and a parlor. There was no bathroom, so the younger children bathed in a tub in the kitchen. Every two weeks, workers hauled in kegs of hot bathwater and came back for the empty kegs the next day. Sigmund and the older girls went to the public baths, like their parents.

Professor Ernst Brücke, Freud's stern mentor.

The new apartment had a long, narrow room that the family called the cabinet. It was for Sigmund alone, a place where he could sleep and study. The cabinet was the only room in the house with an oil lamp. Everyone else had to work by candlelight at night.

Sigmund ate his dinner in the cabinet most evenings, with his books spread open in front of him. And when he brought university chums home, he hurried them into his private room. His sisters scolded him for this—they wanted to meet Sigmund's good-looking friends! His sister Anna commented, "One would have imagined that the presence in the house of five young women would have had some attraction for these young men, but they seemed less interested in entertainment than in scientific discussion with our learned brother."

A typical student at the University of Vienna took his final exams and graduated after five years of study. Sigmund Freud, it seems, was no typical student. When he turned twenty-four, in May 1880, he had spent seven years in university and had yet to earn a degree. His friends teased him, calling him an idler. Relatives asked Amalia and Jacob prying questions: What's the matter with Sigmund?

It was not laziness that held Sigmund back but his "habit of research," he said. He could have remained a student researcher in Brücke's lab for many more years and been quite happy. He saw, though, that he was causing hardship for his family. Jacob Freud never pressured his son to graduate and always gave him pocket change, but there was little money to spare. Jacob was in his mid-sixties now, at an age when many men retire.

Sigmund understood that he needed to get his degree and start earning a salary. So for the next ten months, he studied hard, committing whole passages from his medical texts to memory. On March 30, 1881, he passed his final examinations with a grade of "excellent" and received his diploma.

Freud now worked as a paid researcher in the physiology lab and did a little teaching on the side to bring in extra money. He didn't need much for himself, because books and cigars were the only things he liked to buy. He thought about making a career in medical research, like Professor Brücke.

But in 1882, Brücke sat Sigmund down and explained some hard facts of life. Sigmund showed promise as a researcher, he said. Unfortunately, it would be many years before he earned more than a pittance from his laboratory work. Aware of the tight

The laboratory of the Institute of Physiology, where Freud worked between 1876 and 1882.

finances in the Freud home, Brücke said that Sigmund would be wise to give up research and become a practicing physician. The fees he earned from his patients would make life easier for him and his family.

Sigmund saw the sense in his professor's advice and left the laboratory to prepare for private practice. His heart was heavy, but not too heavy, because he now had his own reason for wanting a larger income: He had fallen in love and was hoping to get married.

One evening in April 1882, Sigmund had come home from work eager to get to his cabinet and his books. He had paused to greet his family, who were seated at the table, and to meet Minna and Martha Bernays, two sisters who were their guests. He took one look at slender, twenty-two-year-old Martha, who was paring an apple, and forgot all about reading. He surprised his family by pulling up a chair and joining in their small talk.

He sent Martha a rose the next day—and every day after that for a month and a half. On May 31, he appeared in person at Martha's door and took her out for a stroll. The romance quickly grew serious. By June 17, the two had promised to marry, but they kept their engagement a secret. Martha's mother, Frau (Mrs.) Emmeline Bernays, was not crazy about this new suitor.

Frau Bernays was a well-to-do widow who looked down on the poorer, less educated Freuds. Martha's father had been a professor, and her grandfather had been a prominent rabbi. Martha's mother wanted a son-in-law with a more distinguished background and better prospects. Frau Bernays objected to something else about Sigmund Freud as well. The Bernays family was religious, and Sigmund called himself an atheist.

Martha and Sigmund exchanged love notes and trinkets

through their friends. He called her Princess, and he cautioned her that their engagement would be a long one. Although he had studied the workings of the human body, he had no experience in treating patients. He would need training in a hospital before he could open an office of his own. He would not be able to afford a home and family for several years.

Sigmund was a jealous fiancé who wanted Martha's love and attention all for himself. He objected to her friendship with other males, even her cousin. And he expected her to obey him just as his family did. He directed Martha to give up her "religious prejudices" and become a nonbeliever. He pressured her to take his side in disagreements with her mother. It is amazing that Martha put up with Sigmund at all.

And Martha's attitude drove Sigmund wild. No matter how firmly he instructed her, she calmly and pleasantly did exactly as she wished. She saw all her friends, practiced her faith, and refused to take part in disputes. Sigmund raged that she was weak-willed and timid, but she stood her ground. She was not about to take orders from Amalia Freud's spoiled son.

Martha had confidence that, given time, Sigmund would learn to value her opinions. Her hunch was correct. Before too long, Sigmund wrote to her, "I observe that I do not gain what I want in you, and I shall lose my loved one if I continue. I have asked of you what is not in your nature, and I have offered you nothing in return." He apologized for trying to control her saying, "One is very crazy when one is in love."

On July 31, 1882, Sigmund Freud started his clinical training at the General Hospital of Vienna. He was about to learn how

Martha Bernays in 1880.

doctors practiced medicine in the late nineteenth century. Hospital training was grueling, just as it is for new doctors today. "Whoever needs more than five hours of sleep should not study medicine," warned one of the teaching physicians.

The hospital was a huge complex covering twenty-five acres, with beds for three thousand patients. People came from all over the Austrian Empire to be treated there, and from as far away as Africa and Asia. If a doctor in training wanted to observe unusual cases, the General Hospital of Vienna was the place to be.

But despite its fine reputation, the hospital was a dirty, drafty place. Surgeons sometimes operated by candlelight, because gas for lighting was in limited supply. On wintry days, patients lay in their wards for many hours in darkness. "And would you believe," Sigmund wrote to Martha, "that there are no polished floors or carpets, and even where ten out of every twenty patients have serious lung diseases, the place is swept out once a day, and the whole room is enveloped in a cloud of dust?"

Doctors were only starting to understand the role of bacteria in illness and infection. The French chemist and biologist Louis Pasteur (1822–95) had recently demonstrated that bacteria invade the body to cause diseases ranging from cholera to tuberculosis. Before Pasteur's work, many people scoffed at the idea of tiny organisms creating illness in vastly larger creatures. Robert Koch (1843–1910), a German scientist, had isolated the germs responsible for anthrax and other illnesses and perfected methods for handling them in research.

Working at the General Hospital of Vienna, the Hungarian doctor Ignaz Semmelweis (1818–65) had discovered how to prevent puerperal, or childbed, fever. This infection of the reproductive tract was killing nearly a third of women who gave birth in

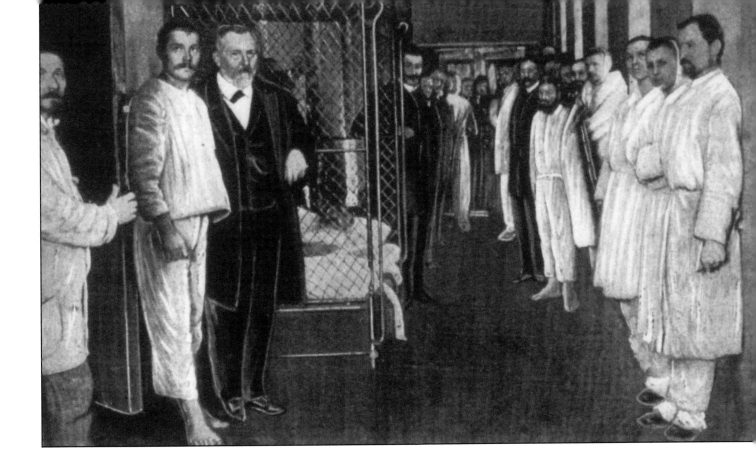

hospital wards. Physicians could lower the rate of infection and death, Semmelweis taught, simply by washing their hands.

Surgeons had reduced the rate of death from infection following operations by cleansing their instruments with carbolic acid, as the British surgeon Joseph Lister (1827–1912) had instructed. But doctors still lacked antibiotics, which would not be discovered until the twentieth century. Any infection that did set in was very tough to treat.

Freud had several weeks' training in one medical specialty and then moved on to another. He decided against becoming a surgeon, because he hated the sight of blood. Psychiatry was not for him either. Freud was appalled to see how psychiatrists misunderstood their patients. At that time, someone with a serious

Richard von Krafft-Ebing, a leading psychiatrist of the late nineteenth century, visits patients in the psychiatric ward of the Vienna General Hospital. Krafft-Ebing was professor of psychiatry at the University of Vienna from 1872 until his death in 1902.

mental illness was likely to be locked away in an asylum with nothing to do, isolated from family and friends. Doctors ignored anything the mentally ill person said, believing that listening would only strengthen the patient's delusions.

Freud tried his hand at internal medicine and dermatology, but the specialty he liked best was neurology, which dealt with diseases of the nervous system. Neurologists saw some of the hospital's strangest cases. For example, Freud examined a teenaged boy, a cobbler's apprentice, with bleeding gums and purplish bruises on his legs—two symptoms of scurvy. The boy also showed troubling signs of a neurological disorder. He could not move his eyes to look in different directions, and he was paralyzed on one side of his body. Before the doctors could form a diagnosis, though, the patient fell into a coma and died.

A weaver with weakened muscles and strange sensory perceptions was another intriguing case. Freud determined that the man suffered from syringomyelia, a rare condition of the spinal cord. Freud treated the man for several weeks, until he was well enough to leave the hospital.

The weaver's case had a successful outcome, but usually neurologists could do little for their patients. Electric shock therapy was the preferred treatment, and Freud learned how to administer it. His patients felt tingling from the shocks, and their muscles twitched.

Medical students at the University of Vienna attend a lecture on the brain.

Electroshock therapy benefits some psychiatric patients even today. In the nineteenth century, however, shock therapy was an inexact science at best. Doctors simply did not know how much electricity was safe or beneficial. Some patients suffered severe burns or died following treatment. In July 1892, the *American Journal of Insanity* warned doctors: "The limit of safety from death or injury from currents of high potential has not yet been determined." It seemed to Freud that speaking to his patients in a kind and soothing manner was much more helpful than treating them with electricity. He felt gratified when the occasional patient improved, enough so to tell Martha, "I have really become a doctor."

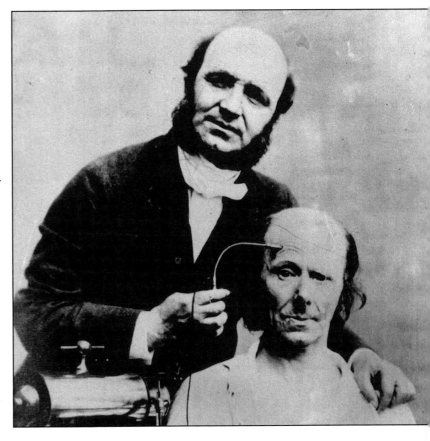

French physician G. B. A. Duchenne de Boulogne (1806–75) pioneered the use of electricity to treat neurological disorders. Here he demonstrates that electric current applied to a patient's forehead causes facial muscles to contract.

Sigmund saw Martha whenever he could. Theirs was not the only romance to unite the Freud and Bernays families. Martha's brother, Eli, was courting Sigmund's sister Anna. On December 26, 1882, Eli and Anna announced their intention to marry. Sigmund and Martha thought the time was right to tell Frau Bernays of their wedding plans as well. Martha's mother took the news calmly and did not forbid the couple to wed. But in the spring of 1883, she moved her family to Wandsbek, a town near Hamburg, Germany, that was far from Vienna and Sigmund Freud.

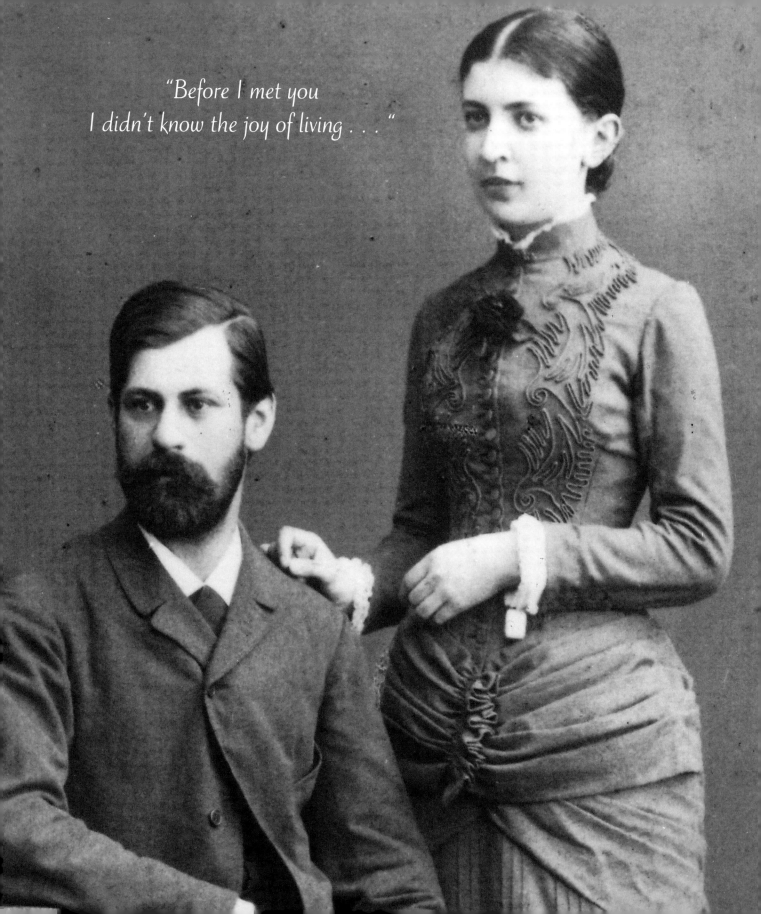

"Before I met you
I didn't know the joy of living . . . "

CHAPTER FOUR

Working, Hoping, Risking

One love letter after another traveled from Vienna to Wandsbek. Sigmund wrote to Martha nearly every night after finishing his work at the hospital. He sent her more than nine hundred letters during the three years they were apart.

In those letters, Sigmund dreamed about the future that he and Martha would share. He imagined "a little home into which sorrow might find its way, but never privation," and he looked forward to feeling "a quiet contentment that will prevent us from ever having to ask what is the point of living." He predicted, "All that has happened and is happening will, by the interest you take in it, become an added interest for me. You will not judge me according to the success I do or do not achieve, but according to my intentions and my honesty."

Sigmund described for Martha his confused mental state after a long day at the hospital: "Strange creatures are billeted in my brain. Cases, theories, diagnostics, formulas have moved into

Sigmund Freud and Martha Bernays in 1885.

brain accommodations most of which have been standing empty . . . here bacteria sometimes live, sometimes turning green, sometimes blue, there come the remedies for cholera. . . . Loudest of all is the cry: tuberculosis? Is it contagious? Is it acquired? Where does it come from?"

Sigmund wrote about himself: "I am very stubborn and very reckless and need great challenges; I have done a number of things which any sensible person would be bound to consider very rash. For example, to take up science as a poverty-stricken man, then as a poverty-stricken man to capture a poor girl—but this must continue to be my way of life: risking a lot, hoping a lot, working a lot." He confided his innermost thoughts: "Before I met you I didn't know the joy of living, and now that 'in principle' you are mine, to have you completely is the one condition I make to life."

Freud was impatient. He racked his brain, desperate for a way to bring in some money and marry Martha sooner. If only he could make a great medical discovery; then he would be an important man, and patients would flock to see him. In 1884, he thought he knew what that discovery would be. He was going to find a medical use for cocaine.

Although even young children now know that cocaine is a dangerous drug, for centuries people believed that it had beneficial effects. During the time of European exploration in the New World, the Incas of Peru chewed the leaves of the coca plant to bring on euphoria and increase alertness. In 1855, European scientists isolated cocaine, the stimulant in coca leaves. The German army carried out experiments with the drug in the 1880s,

In the 1880s, it was legal to buy and use cocaine in the United States, just as it was in Europe. Manufacturers added the drug to a variety of products, including this toothache remedy.

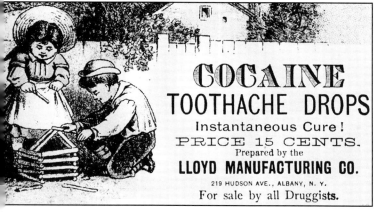

COCAINE
TOOTHACHE DROPS
Instantaneous Cure!
PRICE 15 CENTS.
Prepared by the
LLOYD MANUFACTURING CO.
219 HUDSON AVE., ALBANY, N. Y.
For sale by all Druggists.

and found that soldiers who were exhausted from taking part in practice maneuvers felt renewed energy after using cocaine. Freud sent for a sample of this intriguing substance, which was legal to possess at that time. As soon as it arrived, he started taking it himself, dissolved in water. The drug lifted his spirits, aided his digestion, and, oddly, numbed his tongue.

Full of enthusiasm about cocaine, Freud sent some to Martha in the hope that it would put color in her cheeks. (He worried that she was too pale.) He gave some to his sisters, and he wrote an article for a scientific journal, praising this miraculous drug. He thought about using cocaine to remedy ailments as diverse as diabetes and seasickness, but first he doled some out to his friend Fleischl.

Freud had befriended Ernst von Fleischl-Marxow, an intelligent, good-natured fellow student, when the two worked side by side in Professor Brücke's laboratory. Fleischl had been suffering from chronic medical problems ever since the day he cut his thumb while dissecting a corpse. Bacteria had entered the wound, and an infection had developed and festered. The only way doctors could prevent the infection from spreading was to amputate the thumb.

But with the loss of his thumb, Fleischl's troubles only worsened. He needed further operations to remove neuromas, which were painful lumps of nerve tissue that formed beneath the skin. The infection lingered despite all the surgery, and the hand ached constantly. At times it hurt so much that Fleischl thought about suicide. He started taking morphine, a drug made from opium, to relieve his pain, but he soon became addicted to it. Freud suspected that if Fleischl took cocaine instead of morphine, he could get pain relief and break his addiction.

Freud's doomed friend,
Ernst von Fleischl-Marxow.

For a short while, Fleischl thought that his friend had solved his problems. The cocaine stopped the pain and eased his craving for morphine. Unfortunately, Fleischl and Freud were ignorant of a fact that is widely known today: Although cocaine use does not lead to physical addiction, people can become psychologically dependent on the drug. Within days, Fleischl was consuming larger doses of cocaine, more and more often. He took so much that he started to hallucinate. Terrified, he thought that snakes were slithering over his body.

Freud wrote to Martha immediately, warning her not to use any more cocaine. And he stayed up many nights with Fleischl, who was struggling to break this second drug dependence. (It is sad to note that there was nothing Freud or any other doctor could have done for Fleischl in the nineteenth century. He would die six years later of medical problems resulting from his wounded hand.)

After witnessing the suffering that he had caused his friend, Freud deeply regretted his championing of cocaine. He reproached himself for urging the drug on his loved ones and for singing its praises in print. He humbly put aside his dream of solving a medical riddle with cocaine.

In an odd twist of fate, Dr. Carl Koller, who was training at the General Hospital to be an ophthalmologist, or eye specialist, did discover a medical use for the drug. While Freud was visiting Martha in the fall of 1884, Koller used cocaine as an anesthetic during eye surgery. A trickle of a cocaine solution quickly numbed the eye, allowing physicians to perform operations that had been impossible before. Koller gained the recognition that Freud had dreamed of for himself.

Freud was now sleeping in a room at the hospital and planning to specialize in neurology. He soon knew a great deal about the nervous system; he even gave lectures to visiting doctors on the medulla oblongata. This, the hindmost section of the brain, controls the heart and respiratory system and performs other functions. In the summer of 1884, Freud was put in charge of the neurology department when two doctors left for the countryside to provide aid during a cholera outbreak. He was responsible for 106 patients, ten nurses, and three other doctors in training.

In January 1885, Freud applied to become a docent, or university lecturer. To be a docent was an honor for a young doctor, and it would ensure a successful future as a practicing physician. Professor Brücke gave him a glowing recommendation, writing that "Dr. Freud is a man with a good general education, of quiet and serious character . . . of fine dexterity, clear vision, comprehensive knowledge . . . with the gift for well-organized written expression." Brücke said that Freud possessed the best attributes "of a scientific researcher and of a well-qualified teacher." After passing an oral exam, giving a lecture ("The Medullary Tracts of the Brain"), and being checked out by the police department, Freud was named a docent on September 5.

Much of the time, though, his life as a neurologist was far less eventful. He made his rounds in the hospital and examined patients. Freud saw a number of women who had been diagnosed as hysterics. The word "hysteric" comes from the Greek word *hysterikos,* meaning "of the womb." Many doctors were convinced that a malfunctioning uterus caused a nervous disorder in these patients, although they were at a loss to explain how that happened. A hysteric might complain of numbness or paralysis. She might have seizures, headaches, tremors, and spells of blindness that had no direct medical cause. Most physicians had little interest in treating hysterics, primarily because they had no idea how to help them. The doctors administered electric shocks, prescribed mineral baths, and sent the women on their way.

Freud was confident that science would furnish him with new and better ways to treat his patients. He read with deep interest about a brilliant French researcher who seemed to be making progress. The neurologist Jean-Martin Charcot had transformed a Paris mental hospital, the Salpêtrière, into a leading research center, turning wards into classrooms and laboratories.

In 1885, with his internship at the hospital nearing its end, Freud won a travel scholarship that enabled him to study with the famous Charcot. He impatiently looked forward to the four months, October through January, that he would spend at the Salpêtrière. Even more exciting was the prospect of seeing Martha again. He had arranged to spend six weeks in Wandsbek before proceeding to Paris. Still worrying about Martha's health, he wrote to her, "When I come I am going to fatten you up and kiss some color into your cheeks."

An early print of the Salpêtrière.

The days in Wandsbek passed all too quickly. Sigmund departed with fond memories of Martha and feelings of relief—Frau Bernays was learning to like and understand him at last. He arrived in Paris already missing Martha but ready to work.

The Salpêtrière turned out to be a haphazard group of buildings that had once stored saltpeter, a substance used in making gunpowder. And the renowned Charcot was a solid, strong man with intense powers of concentration. "He used to look again and again at the things he did not understand, to deepen his impression of them day by day," Freud wrote, "till suddenly an understanding of them dawned on him." Charcot's greatest pleasure came from uncovering new knowledge. He was someone, Freud later recalled, "whose personality and whose work none ever approached without learning from them."

Freud watched and listened as Charcot and his assistants examined patients and commented on their conditions. He attended lectures, at which the great Dr. Charcot stood at the front of the room with his hand tucked between the buttons of his coat like the emperor Napoleon.

Charcot alone seemed to be unraveling the mystery of hysteria. He had found that by using hypnosis, he could cause a healthy person to show signs of the disorder. Freud felt a thrill pass through his body when he learned of that discovery. Charcot had demonstrated that the mind played a role in illness and health. What's more, he had identified hysteria in men as well as in women.

Freud was continually challenged in Paris both as a doctor and also as a tourist. He was so taken with the majesty of Notre Dame Cathedral that he climbed its tower not once but twice. He

Jean-Martin Charcot, Freud's teacher and mentor.

attended the opera, and he saw a performance by the great actor Sarah Bernhardt. The play was not very good, Sigmund wrote to Martha, "but how this Sarah can act. After the first words uttered in an intimate, endearing voice, I felt I had known her all my life."

Most inspiring of all, though, were the ancient statues and manuscripts at the Louvre, one of Paris's great art museums. Sigmund described for Martha "Assyrian kings—tall as trees and holding lions for lapdogs in their arms, winged human animals with beautifully dressed hair, cuneiform inscriptions as clear as if they had been done yesterday, and then Egyptian bas-reliefs decorated in fiery colors, veritable colossi [giant statues] of kings, real sphinxes, a dreamlike world."

He returned to Vienna with an artist's print that showed Charcot and some students discussing a patient. He would treasure that souvenir for the rest of his life. He brought back a head full of ideas as well, ideas that frustrated him as he started to practice medicine. He treated people with electrotherapy, baths, and massage, but he had little faith in what he was doing. The remedies, he wrote, "had no more relation to reality than some 'Egyptian' dreambook."

He rented a small suite of offices, and he lived and worked there, sleeping behind a curtain that divided one of the rooms. Fees from his patients dribbled in, and he wondered whether he would ever make enough money to get married. He worried that during the long wait Martha would forget how to laugh.

The engagement might have dragged on for several more years if Martha's relatives had not come to the rescue. Her

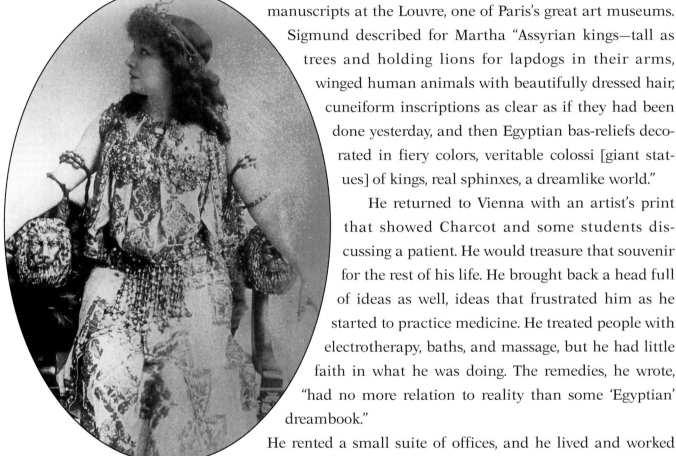

In 1890, Sarah Bernhardt triumphed onstage in CLEOPATRA, a drama written for her by the French playwright Victorien Sardou.

wealthy aunt gave the couple a sum of money, and a kind uncle coughed up some more. Sigmund and Martha now had enough cash to buy furniture and rent an apartment. There was no reason to wait any longer. Sigmund told Martha that "we would need two or three little rooms to live and eat in and to receive a guest, and a stove in which the fire for our meals never goes out."

As soon as he could, Sigmund hopped on a train for Germany. And on September 13, 1886, he and Martha were married in Wandsbek's town hall. The next day, although Sigmund was still a committed atheist, he took part in a traditional Jewish wedding at the Bernays home, because Austria required its citizens to be married in a religious service.

Sigmund Freud was now thirty years old, and Martha was twenty-five. They were grateful and happy to be united at last. Back in Vienna, Sigmund busied himself with his medical practice, and on October 15, he was invited to describe Charcot's work to the Imperial Society of Physicians.

An American manufacturer touted its "nerve pills" as a quick cure for hysteria.

Freud expected his colleagues to embrace the findings that he presented; instead, as he detailed the use of hypnotism at the Salpêtrière, his listeners guffawed. When he went on to describe hysteria in males, a doctor in the audience interrupted to ask, "My dear sir, how can you talk such nonsense?" The doctor pointed out that a patient must have a uterus in order to be a hysteric. It was common knowledge.

LA LEÇON CLINIQUE DU DR. CHARCOT, by Andre Brouillet. Freud treasured his print of this painting and hung it in his office.

Seeing is believing, the doctors said. They challenged Freud to show them a male hysteric. Only with an actual patient in front of them would Vienna's medical community believe what Freud had to say.

So on November 26, Sigmund Freud was back at the lectern, speaking to the same distinguished audience. This time he brought along a patient, a twenty-nine-year-old man who had shown symptoms of hysteria since childhood. "I am far from thinking that what I am showing you is a rare or peculiar case," Freud said. "On the contrary, I regard it as a very ordinary case of frequent occurrence, though one which may often be over-looked." But even with the patient in front of them, the other doctors called male hysteria hogwash. They resolved to keep their distance from Dr. Freud and his odd ideas. One senior colleague went so far as to bar Freud from entering his laboratory.

If that was how the learned men responded to new concepts, Freud decided, he wanted nothing to do with them. He turned away from academic life and stopped going to professional meetings. He devoted himself to his family and was overjoyed when a daughter was born in October 1887. The newborn Mathilde appeared homely to Freud. But as days passed and friends observed that the baby resembled her father, he changed his tune. Before long he remarked, "She has already grown much prettier, sometimes I think already quite pretty."

Freud's thoughts kept returning to the months he had spent in Paris and to Charcot's use of hypnotism. He started to experiment with hypnosis on his own patients. He found that he could rid a hysterical patient of a symptom, for a little while, by putting her in a trance and telling her that the symptom would be gone when she woke up. He was interested to observe that patients under hypnosis could recover memories that were absent from their minds in the waking state.

In the summer of 1889, Freud journeyed to Nancy, in northeastern France, to consult with Hippolyte Bernheim, a leading hypnotist. Bernheim, too, was treating hysterics, but with mixed results. His method had some drawbacks, he said. It was easier to hypnotize some patients than others, and a few patients resisted hypnotism altogether. Also, any relief the patients gained was short-lived. Their symptoms tended to come back once treatment ended.

Still, Sigmund Freud watched in fascination as Bernheim carried out his work. He sensed the presence of "powerful mental processes which nevertheless remained hidden from the consciousness of men." Freud asked himself, What were those unconscious processes? How could they be brought to light?

"When our little Mathilde chuckles we think it is the most beautiful thing that could happen to us . . ."

CHAPTER FIVE

The Talking Cure

A few medical men stayed loyal to Sigmund Freud, and he valued their company more than ever. One close friend was Josef Breuer, a highly respected physician who was fourteen years older than Freud. A kind and generous man, Breuer had loaned money to Freud during his student years and had never pressed for repayment. Knowing of Freud's interest in the unconscious mind, Breuer told his friend the unusual story of a patient he had been treating, a woman he identified as Anna O.

Breuer first saw Anna O. in 1880, when she was twenty-one years old. She had come to him with a classic case of hysteria. She was partially paralyzed, and her vision was oddly impaired. She spoke only in English, insisting that she had forgotten her native German. Her mood changed wildly. She had periods of high spirits followed by spells of anxiety.

Breuer reported that Anna O. suffered from "frightening hallucinations of black snakes, which is how she saw her hair, rib-

Josef Breuer and his wife, Mathilde. Freud, who chose all of his children's names, named his oldest daughter after Mathilde Breuer.

bons, and similar things." She felt as if she had "two selves," Breuer said, "a real one and an evil one which forced her to behave badly." What's more, her symptoms were growing worse. For six weeks she had avoided water, quenching her thirst with fruit instead.

One day, Breuer tried hypnosis on Anna O. While she was in a trance, he asked about her dislike of water, and when exactly it had started. She described a day when she had visited a friend, and how the friend had let a dog drink from her glass. Anna had said nothing at the time, not wanting to be rude, although her friend's behavior disturbed her. Under hypnosis, Anna let loose all the disgust and anger she had felt on that day. Breuer said that what happened next was amazing: "She asked for something to drink, drank a large quantity of water without any difficulty and woke from her hypnosis with the glass at her lips." She never had trouble drinking water again.

Breuer discovered that if he could help Anna recall the first time one of her symptoms appeared and express the emotions triggered at that time, the symptom would vanish, never to return. Breuer named his treatment method catharsis, using a term that is rooted in ancient Greek. "Catharsis" refers to the emotional cleansing that people feel after viewing artistic works such as tragic plays. Anna O. called Breuer's treatment "the talking cure."

(Anna O.'s real name was Bertha Pappenheim. She later became one of the world's first social workers and did much to aid Jewish orphans in Eastern Europe. Although she was never entirely free of hysterical symptoms, she led a useful and rewarding life.)

Freud understood that—almost by chance—Breuer had achieved a breakthrough in the treatment of hysteria. On May 1, 1889, he tried catharsis with one of his own patients, a woman identified in his writings as Frau Emmy von N. And he soon found that he did not need to use hypnosis. Catharsis worked just as well when his patients were fully awake. Locked away in their minds, Freud believed, was complete knowledge about the source of their disorder. "It was only a question of obliging them to communicate it," he wrote. Again and again he asked his patients, "How long have you had this symptom?" "What was its origin?"

If a patient responded with the words "I really don't know," Freud persisted. "I placed my hand on the patient's forehead," he explained, "or took her head between my hands and said, 'You will think of it under the pressure of my hand. At the moment at which I relax my pressure you will see something in front of you or something will come into your head. It will be what we are looking for.'"

He went on treating patients in that manner until the day a woman begged him to be quiet. His questions interrupted the flow of her thoughts, she said. From then on, Freud kept his mouth shut during treatment sessions. He listened with great care while his patients confided their memories, emotions, and ideas.

Freud and other educated Europeans had been taught that thinking ought to proceed logically. Concepts should follow one another in a neat, step-by-step march toward a conclusion. Now, Freud asked his patients to break the rule, to let one idea trigger the next in no obvious order. Later on, the apparent jumble of thoughts and feelings would begin to make sense. He offered only gentle guidance as the patients worked their way from anguish to enlightenment. Freud called this undirected approach free association. He believed that it allowed him to probe deep layers of the unconscious that had remained unexplored.

Breuer spoke admiringly of his friend's accomplishments. "Freud's intellect is soaring at its highest," he wrote to an acquaintance. "I gaze after him as a hen at a hawk."

Why did catharsis and free association help the patients of Breuer and Freud? The two men theorized that hysteria had its roots in troubling events that took place far in a patient's past. Normally, people react to such events with anger or tears. They release their emotions, and mental healing begins. Sometimes, however, the feelings brought on by a traumatic event are too painful or confusing for the person to deal with. Instead of being vented in the normal way, the sorrow and anger are banished to the unconscious region of the mind. Freud said that they are "repressed." But emotions cannot stay bottled up forever. In a process called conversion, they erupt later as physical or psychological symptoms. The goal of treatment was to help patients retrieve their buried emotions and release them in a healthy way.

Freud and Breuer described their findings in a book, *Studies on Hysteria,* which was published in 1895. The book details the treatment of Anna O., Emmy von N., and other patients. "Any experience which calls up distressing affects—such as those of fright, anxiety, shame or physical pain—may operate as a trauma of this kind," the authors told their readers. They described patients who were disabled by memories of those experiences and by emotions that had been buried. "Hysterics suffer mainly from reminiscences," Breuer and Freud wrote.

The concepts presented in the new book excited a small handful of readers. It was thrilling to think "that it may one day become possible to approach the innermost secret of the human personality," wrote a reviewer in a Vienna newspaper. For the most part, though, the medical profession rejected *Studies on Hysteria,* and the public ignored it. In thirteen years, only 626 people bought the book.

Sales may have been poor, but Freud was confident that his ideas would gain acceptance, given time. "I have the distinct feeling that I have touched on one of the great secrets of nature," he stated. He took satisfaction in his achievements—and in his growing family.

Five more children had been born between 1889 and 1895: Martin, Oliver, Ernst, Sophie, and Anna. Martha's sister, Minna Bernays, joined the family group in 1896, after her fiancé died of tuberculosis. Aunt Minna never married. She was a beloved member of the household for more than forty years, helping Martha care for the children and shop for the large family. Intelligent and well read, she grasped the importance of Sigmund's work and had perceptive things to say about it. He soon counted her among his close friends.

In 1891, the Freuds had moved to a roomier apartment in a building at 19 Berggasse. Sigmund ran up and down the stairs from his office on the ground level to his family in their rooms above. He was a doting parent who delighted in his children's games and nursed them when they were ill. Without modern medicines and vaccines, children in the nineteenth century commonly came down with scarlet fever, whooping cough, and other life-threatening diseases. And doctors—even those who were loving fathers—had little to offer in the way of treatment.

Minna Bernays, a beloved member of the Freud household.

The Freud home at 19 Berggasse was in the middle of this Vienna city block.

Little Mathilde almost died from diphtheria at the age of five or six as her desperate parents wondered what in the world they could do for her. Although Mathilde's airway was nearly blocked, she managed to ask for a strawberry. Sigmund scoured the city markets, but strawberries were rare in Vienna at that time of year. He found some at last in a gourmet shop and hurried home with his purchase. Mathilde took one bite from a strawberry and started to cough. The coughing cleared her throat, and she survived.

While Mathilde and her siblings played in the apartment overhead or in the garden behind 19 Berggasse, Sigmund Freud delved further into the nature of the unconscious. He perceived that in this uncharted region of the mind, the rules of logic do not apply. All kinds of thoughts and feelings can be lumped together without any obvious connection. Also, emotions exiled to the unconscious do not weaken with the passing of time, according to Freud. They remain strong and painful indefinitely.

Freud theorized that the unconscious mind can think, but that it forms thoughts in images rather than in words. He said that the unconscious employs symbols, using objects to stand for other objects or for ideas. It seemed to him that the unconscious has trouble separating fantasy from reality. An experience that is vividly imagined can seem just as real to the unconscious as one that actually happened.

As Freud continued to study people with hysteria, he noticed that many of the traumas his patients described were sexual in nature. Haltingly, reluctantly, one patient after another told of sexual abuse in early childhood. The abusers were servants, friends, and relatives—frequently the patients' own fathers.

Listening to these painful stories, Freud traced other neuroses, or emotional disorders, to sexual seduction in childhood. This kind of abuse seemed to be a key cause of psychological problems. Freud wrote two articles for scientific journals describing his new seduction theory of mental illness. He published his findings even though he knew that most doctors would be outraged to read them.

The physicians of Freud's day avoided the awkward subject of sex when dealing with their patients. Freud lived in a period of history when people clothed themselves from the neck to the ankles, when body parts were not mentioned by name in polite conversation. As Freud expected, doctors promptly discounted the seduction theory, and they ridiculed its author. "In those days, when one mentioned Freud's name in a Viennese gathering, everyone would begin to laugh as if someone had told a joke," said a man who lived in the city at that time.

The seduction theory was too much even for Josef Breuer to accept. As Freud placed greater importance on sexual matters, Breuer feared that he had made a mistake in working so closely with the younger man. He thought that Freud was straying dangerously from the path of scientific study, and he worried that his own reputation would suffer as a result. He began to avoid Sigmund Freud in both his social and his professional life.

Without Breuer at his side, Freud was left to carry on his work in "splendid isolation," he said. He viewed himself as a heroic man of science exploring unknown territory on his own.

He was not truly alone, though, because he had formed a friendship with another doctor. Wilhelm Fliess was a nose and throat specialist in Berlin who liked nothing better than to sit and talk for hours, playing with ideas. Fliess had come up with a theory of bisexuality that is still taken seriously today. He proposed that every man and woman has feelings and physical urges in common with the opposite sex. In other words, some aspects of every human personality are masculine, and some are feminine.

Fliess also had a strong interest in numerology, which is the belief that numbers influence people's lives and the future. He concocted a notion, now regarded as nonsense, that the numbers 28, 23, 5, and 51 govern much of human life.

Sigmund Freud and Wilhelm Fliess.

When the two men got together in Vienna or Berlin, Freud told Fliess all about his treatment method, which he now called psychoanalysis, and the seduction theory. Putting his thoughts into words helped him make sense of them. Freud revealed to Fliess how important his work had become to him. "I hope to be occupied with scientific interests to the end of my life," he admitted. "Apart from them I am scarcely a human being any longer." With Breuer out of his life, Freud looked to Fliess for assurance.

Soon, Freud lost the companionship of someone else close to him. Jacob Freud died on October 23, 1896, at the age of eighty. To Sigmund, a father's death was "the most important event, the most poignant loss, in a man's life." He felt profound sorrow, and he understood for the first time how deeply he had loved and admired the old wool merchant. He remembered his father in a letter to Wilhelm Fliess. "With that combination of deep wisdom and romantic lightheartedness peculiar to him he had meant a great deal to me," Freud wrote. He understood that toward the end, his father had lost interest in everyday events. But that knowledge brought no comfort. He noted, "His life had been over a long time before he died, but his death seems to have aroused in me memories of all the early days." He concluded, "I now feel quite uprooted."

Freud's early memories were much on his mind, and he began a daring project: the analysis of his own psyche. He spent part of each day reliving childhood events and examining how they had shaped his later life. It took courage and rare honesty to confront the dark side of his personality. He had to face up to

Jacob Freud, in a photograph taken near the end of his life.

fears and urges that most people hide from themselves. This, however, was a task that needed to be done. Freud believed that he would never have a full understanding of his patients' mental processes until he had fathomed his own.

The self-analysis was often rough going. There were "days when I slink about oppressed because I have not been able to understand anything," Freud told Fliess. But there were also "days in which a flash illuminates the connections and enables one to comprehend what has gone before."

Looking at his childhood through the lens of self-analysis, Freud saw that as a young boy he had felt intense love and longing for his mother. At the same time, he had resented his father, the man who shared his mother's bed and received so much of her affection. He had made a wish he dared not act upon, a wish to banish his father from the home and possess his mother completely.

Oedipus Complex

Freud came to believe that all children between the ages of four and six form a strong attachment to the parent of the opposite sex. This attachment resembles an adult's feeling toward his or her mate. The child views the parent of the same sex as a rival, yet is powerless to act on these frightening drives. How well the child overcomes the attachment and the fears and fantasies it evokes, Freud said, will influence his or her relationships in adult life.

Freud found a name for this psychological conflict in the tragedy *Oedipus Tyrannus,* by the ancient Greek dramatist Sophocles. Oedipus, in Greek mythology, is a king of Thebes who unknowingly kills his father and marries his mother. He acts out what the young child only imagines. Learning the truth drives Oedipus to despair and death.

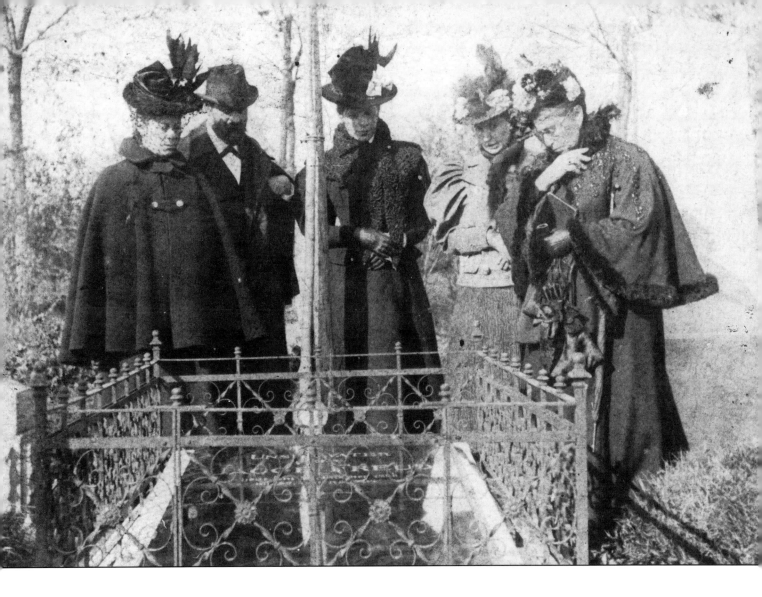

"The Greek myth seizes on a compulsion which everyone rec-
ognizes because he has felt traces of it in himself," Freud wrote.
"Every member of the audience was once a budding Oedipus in
phantasy, and this dream-fulfilment played out in reality causes
everyone to recoil in horror." Explaining that each male was fated
"to direct our first sexual impulses toward our mothers and our
first impulses of hatred and violence toward our fathers," Freud
called these connected emotions the Oedipus complex. He named

*Freud visits his father's grave
with his mother (far right)
and three of his sisters.*

the parallel feelings in girls (desire for the father and rivalry with the mother) the Electra complex. Electra is a figure in Greek mythology who avenged the death of her father, King Agamemnon, after he was murdered by her mother.

Once he had identified these complexes, Freud reflected on his patients' reports of childhood seduction. So many of the stories he heard sounded like fantasies to him now. He saw them as the imaginings of very young girls wishing to capture their fathers' affection. After all, he recognized his own early desire for his mother, yet he knew that no physical union had ever taken place.

This has become one of the most controversial aspects of Freudian thought. Today, many psychologists take issue with Freud's assumption that his patients' memories of childhood abuse were imagined. They assert that the sexual abuse of children is all too common now, and that no doubt it was in Freud's time as well. Other mental health professionals question whether the memories reported by Freud's patients have any validity at all. They point out that by asking the right questions, a therapist can cause a patient both to create false memories and to be convinced that they are real. In fact, the American Medical Association warned in 1994 that memories of childhood sexual abuse recovered in adulthood should be treated as suspect unless they can be verified. (The warning applies only to "recovered" memories, not to those that have remained with a person since the time of abuse.) It is possible that Freud unknowingly coaxed his patients into telling him what he wanted to hear.

The origin of the memories reported by Freud's patients will remain an open question. Freud concluded, though, that his patients were unable to separate real memories from fanciful ones. And to the unconscious, he believed, the two were one and the same.

In time, Freud would look upon this moment of understanding as an important step forward. But for now, he felt like a failure. He decided that the seduction theory, which had taken up so much of his time and exposed him to ridicule, was false. Vienna laughed at him all over again when he admitted his mistake. In Freud's view, though, the confession had to be made if he wanted to pursue the truth.

"This first account may be compared
to an unnavigable river . . ."

CHAPTER SIX

The "Royal Road"

When Sigmund Freud saw a patient for the first time, he listened to the story of the person's life and illness. "This first account may be compared to an unnavigable river whose stream is at one moment choked by masses of rock and at another divided and lost among shallows and sandbanks," he explained. Errors and gaps in the story were the masses of rock. Facts withheld on purpose formed the shallows and sandbanks. Freud's task in the months of treatment ahead was to clear the river of debris. He helped patients fill in missing information so that their stories flowed clearly from childhood to the present. Through psychoanalysis, he helped patients understand the impact of earlier events.

Freud noticed that patients struggling to find order in their lives frequently recounted their dreams. Free association brought dreams to mind so often that his curiosity was aroused. There had to be a connection between a patient's problems and the

dream world, no matter how strange and illogical the dreams seemed to be.

Freud had long been intrigued by the bizarre images that ran through his mind during sleep. "I have such unruly dreams," he wrote to Martha when they were engaged. As a boy, he had recorded his dreams in a notebook. Now he paid close attention to them again.

Human beings have always tried to explain their dreams. Many peoples of the world, both past and present, have believed that dreams come from the supernatural world, that they are prompted by gods, spirits, or demons. The ancient Greeks believed that dreams carried coded messages from the gods and that they entered the body through its pores. Artemidorus Daldianus, a Roman living in the second century, traveled the known world to study the literature of dreams and concluded that dreams were instructions from the spirit world.

The Europeans of Freud's time thought that dreaming was a natural phenomenon but meaningless. It was commonly said that dreams resulted from indigestion, from feeling too hot or too cold, or from smelling a strong odor while asleep. Some people insisted that dreams offered an escape from waking life. Others disagreed, saying that trivial events from daily life constantly popped up in their dreams. They claimed to enjoy no escape at all.

Freud suspected that dreams were more than upset stomachs or bits of experience floating through the sleeping mind. He wrote, "The dream is not meaningless, not absurd, does not imply that one part of our store of ideas is dormant while another part begins to awake." He was sure that dreams have a purpose, because they are an activity carried out by a complex mind. But what was their purpose? What did they mean? Those were the questions that needed to be answered.

Freud believed that he uncovered a dream's hidden meaning for the first time in July 1895, while vacationing with his family at the Schloss Belle Vue, a lodge in the hills outside Vienna. He had a strange dream one night about a patient who had stopped treatment before being cured. She was a woman he identified as Irma.

In the dream as Freud related it, Irma comes to a party looking pale and puffy. He tells her, "If you still have pains, it is really only your own fault." Irma replies, "If you only knew what pains I have in the throat, stomach, and abdomen—I am choked by them." Worried that he has overlooked a physical ailment in his patient, Freud peers into her throat, where he sees strange scabs and curly bones. Not knowing what to make of this finding, he consults several colleagues. They tell him that Irma has an infection, and that she caught it when another doctor gave her a shot, probably with a dirty needle.

Freud used free association to decipher this dream. Just as his patients discovered links between random thoughts and feelings, he found elements in the dream that reminded him of other people and events. For example, his examination of Irma's throat brought to mind a medical case he had learned of several days earlier. The patient was a woman who had destroyed her nasal passages with cocaine. This memory then led him to recall his friend Fleischl and the sad outcome of his cocaine use.

Freud had been relieved, in the dream, to learn that Irma's symptoms resulted from an infection and not from the failure of his treatment. After a long analysis of its content, he detected a wish hidden behind his dream. It was a wish not to be responsible for the suffering of others—Irma, Fleischl, or anyone else.

Freud put it this way: "The dream represents a certain state of affairs, such as I might wish to exist; *the content of the dream is thus the fulfilment of a wish; its motive is a wish.*"

Anxious to study other dreams, Freud asked his wife and children to describe theirs. "It was unusual for him to discuss his work in the family circle; but this was something of an exception," his son Martin stated. "We had all been told about it, and he even encouraged us to tell him of our dreams: something we did with enthusiasm. He even explained to us in simple language what could be understood of dreams, their origin and meaning."

In every dream he analyzed, Freud observed the same pattern. It appeared to him that the dream world is a place where wishes come true. He explained that as a person falls asleep, the conscious part of the mind relaxes. Long-held wishes are then free to emerge from the unconscious. As dreaming proceeds, the wishes are fulfilled.

Freud said that these wishes are unknown, and may be unacceptable, to the conscious, waking self. For that reason, they arrive cloaked in a disguise. Every object, event, or person in a dream stands for something or someone else. The details a person remembers when awake are symbols that hide the underlying meaning of the dream. Freud believed that by decoding this symbolic language he had found the *via regia*, or royal road, "to a knowledge of the unconscious element in our psychic life."

He was certain that he had made an important discovery. "Insight such as this falls to one's lot but once in a lifetime," he said. He viewed dream interpretation as a valuable tool for exploring the unconscious, one that could help millions of people gain self-knowledge. Also, dreaming was a natural process that occurred in people with good mental health. Dream interpretation, then, was "the starting point of a new and deeper science of the mind." Freud said that understanding dreams would shed light on how normal minds worked. He imagined a future day when a plaque might hang at the Schloss Belle Vue to inform visitors, "Here the secret of dreams was revealed to Dr. Sigm. Freud on July 24, 1895."

Over the next few years, Freud studied hundreds of dreams—his patients', his family's, and his own. He gathered his findings in a book, *The Interpretation of Dreams,* published in 1899. Freud picked apart many dreams in this book, revealing the wishes that he thought prompted them. The wishes varied widely, from his own desire to be innocent of causing pain, to the common yearning to see dead relatives alive again. "Even dreams with a painful content are to be analyzed as wish fulfilments," Freud wrote. In such a case the wish might be a desire to gain revenge, or to be punished for past acts. Freud went on to state that "everyone has wishes which he would not like to confess to others, which he does not care to admit even to himself."

During sleep, these and other wishes sprout from the unconscious like mushrooms, Freud said. A dream may even be sparked by something as simple as the wish to stay in bed. How many students have dreamed of waking and dressing for school while snoozing through their alarm bell?

Through his interpretation of dreams, Freud attempted to show that people are often unaware of the thought processes going on in their own minds. As he explained, "The most complex mental operations are possible without the cooperation of consciousness."

Freud's dream studies are another aspect of his work that has been criticized in recent decades. Scholarly research has revealed

The title page of THE INTERPRETATION OF DREAMS, *first published in 1899. The Latin quotation is from the Roman poet Virgil: "If I cannot bend Heaven, then I will stir Hell."*

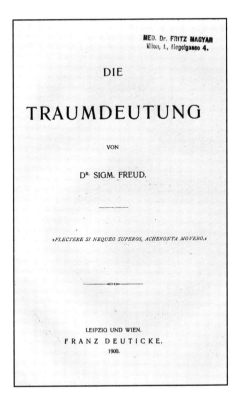

that Freud sometimes held back information that was embarrassing or that contradicted his conclusions. For example, he never disclosed that the woman appearing in his famous dream about Irma had been a patient of his friend Wilhelm Fliess. She had suffered severe bleeding after Fliess bungled an operation on her nasal cavity and left a piece of surgical gauze inside her head. It is likely that these events influenced the meaning of Freud's dream.

Despite the criticism, many people still call *The Interpretation of Dreams* Freud's major contribution to psychology and one of the great books of Western civilization. It has been reprinted many times and translated into numerous languages. But at first, the book's importance was not obvious. Very few copies were sold—just 351 in six years. The educated people of Vienna saw dream analysis as one more crackpot idea from Dr. Sigmund Freud. "Freud was that queer fellow who . . . imagined himself an interpreter of dreams," recalled Max Graf, a musicologist who later became Freud's friend. "More than that, he was the man who saw sex in everything. It was considered bad taste to bring up Freud's name in the presence of ladies."

The scorned doctor consoled himself by saying, "They may abuse my doctrines by day, but I am sure they dream of them by night." He continued to welcome patients who believed that medicine had failed them.

Freud had always been tolerant of public opinion, believing his ideas needed time to gain acceptance. Even now, he wrote to Wilhelm Fliess, "The time is not ripe for followers. There is too much that is new and incredible, and too little strict proof." Yet he felt discouraged. He had hoped *The Interpretation of Dreams* would bring him some respect.

Sigmund Freud was forty-four years old. Most men his age

had established their careers, but he was still struggling to be recognized. And his friendship with Fliess, which had been a refuge, was falling apart. The nose and throat specialist accused Freud of taking credit for the theory of bisexuality. Freud insisted that there had been a misunderstanding, but Fliess held a grudge.

Family life had always offered comfort, and it did so now. Freud came home to eat lunch with the family every day, unless they were having chicken or cauliflower, two foods he hated. He visited his mother and sisters on Sundays, and he looked forward to summer vacations, when he hiked with the children in the mountains. In May or June, Martha and Minna packed up the children's clothes and toys and took the youngsters to the Schloss Belle Vue hotel or to a farmhouse in Bavaria, a forested region

Anna and Sophie Freud.

of southern Germany. Sigmund broke away from his work later in the season to join the family.

Freud may have been his mother's jewel, but he had no favorites among his own children. He enjoyed them as individuals and watched with interest as their personalities developed. Levelheaded Mathilde helped her mother and aunt look after the young ones. Sophie, the prettiest of Freud's daughters, liked to dress fashionably. Martin and Ernst were close friends who skated, skied, and sailed together.

Martin was reckless; several times he came home limping after a fall on the snowy slopes. Oliver, unlike his brothers, preferred mathematics and drawing to sports. He drew maps of the mountain terrain while on vacation and diagrammed Vienna's railroad lines at home. Anna, the youngest, was a sassy little girl who turned serious as she grew older. She took up knitting and made it a lifelong hobby. Convinced that she would never be as pretty as Sophie, Anna paid no attention to fashion. She often wore traditional Austrian dresses with full skirts and aprons.

Oliver, Martin, and Ernst Freud.

Anna Freud remembered her father as "even tempered, optimistic, and even gay." While on vacation, Freud became something of a child himself when he and the children searched the woods for wild mushrooms. Martin Freud described his father's joy upon finding a choice specimen. "He would run to it and fling his hat over it before giving a shrill signal on the flat silver whistle he carried in his waistcoat pocket," Martin wrote. "We would all rush towards the sound of the whistle, and only when the concentration was complete would father remove the hat and allow us to inspect and admire the spoil."

The family vacations were jolly times, but Freud longed to journey beyond the Vienna woods. Martha was too busy with the children to travel with him, so in 1898, he toured Italy with his brother, Alexander. The two men browsed in shopping arcades in the medieval center of the city of Bologna. They viewed famous art collections in Florence, and they cruised the canals of Venice in

flat-bottomed gondolas. In Padua, Sigmund was fascinated to see many art objects dating from ancient times.

Two years later, while visiting Innsbruck, Austria, he bought a Roman statue. It was the first of many antiquities that Freud acquired over the years. He perceived a unique beauty in his collection of relics. "The things put me in high spirits and speak of distant times and lands," he said. Studying his treasures, he felt close to the people of past civilizations. He arranged the collection on his desk so that he could see it while analyzing patients.

Sigmund and Alexander Freud took other trips together. In Greece, they gazed at ruins so awe-inspiring that Sigmund won-

A family party. Martin Freud stands beside his father. Seated, left to right, are Ernst, Sophie, Martha Freud, Anna, Minna Bernays, and Oliver.

dered briefly whether he might be imagining them. In 1901, the brothers visited Rome, a city Sigmund loved more than any other. Like countless tourists, he tossed a coin into the Fountain of Trevi and marveled at the ceiling of the Sistine Chapel, painted by Michelangelo. He would return to Rome six times. "What a pity one can't live here always!" he lamented in one of his many letters home.

Every year, when summer ended, Freud returned to the routine of work. He woke early on weekdays and saw his first patient at eight A.M. He was still at his desk writing books, articles, and letters long after the children were asleep.

Freud was a creature of habit. He took a break from his work every afternoon to walk along Vienna's Ringstrasse, a tree-lined boulevard that wrapped around the heart of the city. He passed the emperor's palace and the opera house, pausing only to buy cigars or to pop in at the barbershop. Freud was fussy about his appearance and had his beard and hair trimmed daily. Sometimes he relaxed by playing cards with friends from the B'nai B'rith society. He belonged to this Jewish service organization, even though he held no religious beliefs, because he felt at home chatting with men who shared his heritage. He remained a member of B'nai B'rith for life.

Psychoanalysis was never far from Freud's thoughts, even when he was at play. He was perfecting his "science of unconscious mental processes" and searching for ways to help his patients. "In every instance the treatment makes heavy claims upon both the physician and the patient," he stated. "Nevertheless, all the trouble involved is as a rule rewarded by the results." He went on to say that the "results of psychoanalysis depend upon the replacement of unconscious mental acts by conscious ones."

Freud labeled one kind of unconscious act transference. He observed that many patients develop strong feelings about their analyst early in treatment, feelings either of love or of hostility. The emotions are too powerful to arise from the doctor-patient relationship alone. Freud thought that his patients were really feeling love or anger toward a parent. They were transferring the emotion onto their doctor, because they viewed him as a parental

Vienna's Ringstrasse, where Freud took his midday walks. The building adorned with statues is the Imperial Opera House.

figure. Freud stated that by exploring their transference, his patients better understood the unconscious drives behind their actions and feelings.

As the twentieth century got under way, Sigmund Freud's isolation came to an end. He was publishing scientific articles and lecturing weekly at the university, and people were starting to pay attention. Doctors and medical students now enjoyed his lectures, although many still objected to his ideas.

Freud had a relaxed, chatty lecturing style, and the students felt free to ask questions. He knew his subject so well that he rarely spoke from notes. During one lecture, he displayed a picture of a man blowing on an electric light, trying to extinguish it. Doctors who treated the symptoms of hysteria as if they were purely physical ailments made a similar mistake, he said. "If you attack the symptom directly, you act in the same way as this man. You must look for the switch"—for the mental disturbance that triggers the symptoms.

Two physicians, Max Kahane and Rudolf Reitler, were excited by Freud's lectures. Dr. Wilhelm Stekel, who had been greatly impressed by *The Interpretation of Dreams,* was another admirer. In 1902, Stekel urged Freud to start a discussion group. Freud was delighted with the idea, so he invited the three men to his office on Wednesday nights to talk about psychoanalysis. He asked another doctor, Alfred Adler, to join them as well. Adler was an ophthalmologist who had a strong interest in the mind. Upon first reading Freud, he had burst out, "This man has something to say to us!"

The Wednesday Psychological Society got off to a happy start. The men debated many topics, from the Oedipus complex to dreams to the unconscious reasons for smoking cigars. "We were like pioneers in a newly discovered land, and Freud was the leader," Stekel recalled. "A spark seemed to jump from one mind to the other, and every evening was like a revelation." Each of Freud's first four admirers went on to practice psychoanalysis.

In the same year, 1902, the Austrian government granted the title of professor to Sigmund Freud. The title was largely a ceremonial honor, accorded to persons of learning, but it was an honor long in coming. Freud knew of many others who had gained the title at younger ages and with fewer accomplishments. Still, he gladly received his friends' good wishes. He joked that the emperor of Austria "had officially recognized the role of sexuality, the Council of Ministers had confirmed the importance of dreams, and the necessity of a psychoanalytic treatment of hysteria had been passed in parliament with a two-thirds majority." But neither Austria nor the rest of the world was ready to embrace Freud's ideas so completely.

"If I am Moses, then you are Joshua. . ."

CHAPTER SEVEN

Prophet

In 1901, Sigmund Freud at last published a book that the public wanted to read. *The Psychopathology of Everyday Life* attempted to explain the slips of the tongue and memory lapses that everyone experiences. Readers had fun discovering what simple errors, such as forgetting someone's name or breaking a dish, might teach them about their unconscious thoughts and wishes.

People reveal much about themselves by doodling, fiddling with their clothing, or humming a tune, Freud said. These actions "have a meaning, generally easy and sure to interpret." He believed that unstudied behavior expresses the same unconscious motives he had described in other writings: the "repressed wishes and complexes which we have learned to know already as the creators of symptoms and dreams."

Another book, published in 1905, was far less popular. In fact, it inspired more disapproval than anything else Freud had written. In *Three Essays on the Theory of Sexuality*, he summed up his

In this mural by John Singer Sargent, Moses stands between the prophet Elijah and Joshua.

thinking about the development of sexual instincts. He shocked his readers by claiming that all infants are born with sexual impulses.

When Freud spoke about sexual gratification, he meant that people feel pleasant sensations when they satisfy physical desires. For example, an infant derives pleasure from stimulation of the mouth. That is why newborns have a strong urge to suck, Freud said, and why older babies put objects in their mouths. At the approximate age of eighteen months, the anus becomes the chief source of sensual pleasure. This is the age at which the child begins to control his or her bowel movements. According to Freud, a third stage of development occurs between the ages of three and six, when the child engages in self-stimulation of the genitals.

Freud said that following this third, or "phallic," stage, children enter a period of "latency." They focus their energy on school and social development, and sexual feelings are repressed. These impulses reawaken at puberty, when the body takes on an adult appearance, and they are directed toward someone outside the family, in the wider world where the child will one day seek a mate.

Today, few people would claim that sexuality suddenly appears for the first time at adolescence. It is widely accepted that sexuality is always part of human nature, and that it evolves slowly, as a person grows and matures. Sexual urges are viewed as natural, and not as something dirty or shameful. At the start of the twentieth century, though, people found Freud's theory of child sexuality deeply distressing. Freud seemed to be challenging the notion that children were morally pure and innocent. In Europe and in America, readers labeled this new book pornography. Dr. Silas Weir Mitchell, a prominent American neurologist, dismissed the book as filth.

After listening to so much criticism, Freud was grateful, one wintry Sunday in 1907, to answer a friendly knock at his door. A psychiatrist named Carl Jung had traveled from Switzerland to Vienna to meet the doctor he greatly admired. Jung had read *The Interpretation of Dreams,* and he had been using psychoanalysis with his patients in Zurich.

Jung had so much to tell Freud that he talked for three hours, barely pausing to take a breath. "Freud was the first man of real importance I had encountered," Jung later recalled. "There was nothing the least trivial in his attitude. I found him extremely intelligent, shrewd, and altogether remarkable."

The tall young doctor in gold-rimmed glasses impressed Freud, too. Jung held his body stiffly, but his mind was flexible enough to embrace new ideas. When the two men finally said good night at two A.M., they were already friends. They continued their dialogue in many letters sent between Vienna and Zurich.

Freud was sure that Jung would be his "son and heir," the person to carry on his work in the future, after his death. At fifty-one, Freud thought that he might not live to see his ideas widely adopted. He compared himself to Moses, the Old Testament prophet who led the Israelites out of captivity in Egypt. According to the Bible, Moses died before his people reached their Promised Land. But he turned over leadership of the Israelites to Joshua, a war hero, before his death.

Freud wrote to Jung, "If I am Moses, then you are Joshua and will take possession of the promised land of psychiatry, which I shall only be able to glimpse from afar." He imagined that Jung might write his obituary one day, and he instructed the younger man "to bear witness that all the opposition has not once succeeded in diverting me from my purpose."

When the Wednesday discussion group grew into the International Psychoanalytic Association, in 1910, Freud named Jung as its president. The organization now had more than twenty members from varied backgrounds. They included Otto Rank, a quiet young man who had worked in a bottle factory; Hanns Sachs, a layperson who had attended Freud's university lectures; and Max Eitingon, a medical student who took walks with Freud and engaged him in lively conversation. Sándor Ferenczi, a congenial doctor from Hungary, was another newcomer to the group. He wore pince-nez, old-fashioned eyeglasses that clipped onto his nose, and he would become one of Freud's closest associates. Freud also had two English-speaking doctors among his followers: Ernest Jones, a Welshman, and Abraham Brill, an American.

And there was someone else who took an interest in psychoanalysis. Anna, the Freuds' youngest child, liked to listen in on meetings of the association from her perch on a low rung of a library ladder. Freud never stifled his children's curiosity and always encouraged them to pursue their interests, whatever those interests might be. Recalling his childhood, Martin Freud said, "We were never ordered to do this, or not to do that; we were never told not to ask questions." Anna therefore knew that she was welcome at the meetings.

In 1909, Freud and Jung, the Moses and Joshua of psychoanalysis, journeyed to the United States. They had been invited to speak at Clark University in Worcester, Massachusetts, to mark the school's twentieth birthday. Freud asked Sándor Ferenczi, his Hungarian friend, to come along. The three men set sail on August 21, full of anticipation.

Their ship docked in Manhattan six days later. Freud and his companions spent a week seeing the sights of New York City.

They strolled in Central Park, the first large urban park in America, and they visited the seaside amusement parks of Coney Island. They elbowed their way through the overcrowded streets of New York's Lower East Side, a neighborhood teeming with immigrants from eastern and southern Europe. One million people were entering the United States at the Ellis Island immigration center every year, and a quarter of them were settling in New York.

The city had so much to offer. Freud admired the antiquities at the Metropolitan Museum of Art, while Ferenczi got a kick out of seeing motion pictures for the first time. New Yorkers liked going to the movies so much that the city had enough movie theaters to seat 150,000 people.

The men traveled by boat and train to Massachusetts, where the president of Clark University greeted them warmly. Freud was moved when the university awarded him an honorary doctorate. "In Europe I felt as though I were despised; but [in the United States] I found myself well received by the foremost men as an equal," he said. "It seemed like the realization of some incredible day-dream: psychoanalysis was no longer a product of delusion, it had become a valuable part of our reality."

Freud delivered five lectures on psychoanalysis at Clark even though he had brought no notes and had given no thought to what he would say. Each morning, he walked for half an hour and came up with an idea for that day's talk.

Freud lectured in German, a language understood by many educated Americans at that time. His audience saw a tidy, bearded man whose hair was starting to turn gray. Freud was constantly alert. His eyes scanned the hall to be sure that every listener kept up with his train of thought.

In September 1909, members of the psychology department at Clark University assembled to be photographed with their European guests. Freud is in the front row, fourth from the right. Carl Jung stands third from the right.

In one lecture, he used an analogy to explain the intense emotions of hysteria. He asked his listeners to imagine a present-day Londoner filled with grief over the death of Eleanor of Aquitaine in the thirteenth century, and another weeping over the Great Fire of 1666. It would be strange, he said, for people to be devastated by events occurring so long in the past. "Now hystericals and all neurotics behave like these two unpractical Londoners," he continued, "not only in that they remember the painful experiences of the distant past, but because they are still strongly affected by them. They cannot escape from the past and neglect present reality in its favor."

From Massachusetts, Freud, Jung, and Ferenczi went to Niagara Falls, which was a spectacle larger and more magnificent than Freud had imagined. They visited James Putnam, a noted neurologist, at his vacation home in the Adirondack Mountains of New York State.

The mountain views reminded him of the Vienna woods, but Freud found little to like about this place or anywhere else in the United States. American food upset his stomach, and the American people were too relaxed in their dealings with others. Freud preferred the formal manners of Europe. Upon his return, he told his British friend Ernest Jones, "America is a mistake; a gigantic mistake, it is true, but none the less a mistake."

The trip to America, though, was anything but a mistake for Sigmund Freud. The *American Journal of Psychology* published his five Clark University lectures. His ideas were widely discussed, which increased his fame and raised his professional stature.

Back home in Vienna, Freud saw new patients with unusual case histories. He treated a wealthy Russian whom he called the Wolf Man in his writings. As a child, this young man had suffered from an irrational fear of wolves that began with a nightmare at the age of four. The phobia disappeared when the patient turned seventeen, only to be replaced by other mental disturbances. With Freud's help, the Wolf Man traced his problems to a memory of seduction by his sister, either real or imagined, and to other early sexual encounters.

Freud published more books, including one that applied psychoanalysis to the life of the great artist

Freud was one of thousands of tourists to view Niagara Falls in the early 1990s. This photograph was taken in 1904.

Martha and Sigmund Freud, a comfortable middle-class couple of the early twentieth century.

and inventor Leonardo da Vinci. Beginning with Leonardo's only reported memory of childhood, Freud attempted to show how his early experiences led to outstanding contributions in science and art.

In *Totem and Taboo,* which was published in 1913, Freud traveled in his imagination to prehistoric times and meditated on the origins of religion. Charles Darwin had speculated that early humans lived in small groups headed by a dominant male. Freud now took this idea a step further. As younger males in the group reached maturity, he said, they challenged the leadership of this older man and perhaps were driven to kill him. The murder of the tribe's father figure would inspire guilt in the living. They would then perform animal sacrifices to atone for the crime, and in so doing symbolically reenact the death scene. Over many years, the murdered leader would be elevated to the status of Supreme Being, and the animal sacrifice would turn into a religious ritual.

The early tribal clash that Freud described was strikingly similar to the conflicting emotions he believed young children feel toward their parents. Near the end of his book, Freud remarked that "the beginnings of religion, morality, social life and art [meet] in the Oedipus complex."

The mind of Sigmund Freud was reaching into new areas of thought, and interest in his work was growing. Psychoanalytical societies were formed in Zurich, Berlin, London, Budapest, and the United States. Lou Andreas-Salomé, a German writer of Russian heritage, came to Vienna in 1911 to study with Freud. She became a psychoanalyst and his lifelong friend.

All in all, life was good. Freud wrote about the path he had chosen in a 1910 letter to his boyhood friend Eduard Silberstein. "I can only say that I encountered many unforeseen labors, that I found unexpectedly a great deal of work; however, on the whole, I am not dissatisfied with the outcome. . . . My scientific expectations are slowly materializing. I am earning as much as we need; in fact, I could have been a well-to-do man had I not preferred to have a large family."

Sigmund and Martha were proud of the way their family had grown. Their oldest daughter, Mathilde, had married in 1910. Sophie Freud married in 1913 and settled with her husband, Max Halberstadt, in Hamburg. In 1914, Sophie gave birth to Sigmund and Martha's first grandchild, a boy named Ernst.

Freud would have felt completely happy if there had not been dissent among his followers. Alfred Adler, the ophthalmologist who was one of the first to join Freud's inner circle, withdrew from the psychoanalytic association in 1911. Adler now rejected Freud's theories of the mind in favor of his own. To Adler's way of thinking, parents were the major influence on a child's development. Faulty parenting led to a condition called the inferiority complex, in which a person repeatedly tries to compensate for feelings that he or she is worth little. Adler thought that aggression and the desire for dominance governed human relations to a greater extent than sexuality did.

Wilhelm Stekel, another early adherent, also left the fold, claiming that in some ways his understanding surpassed Freud's.

Freud was sorry to see the men go, although he acknowledged their right to pursue their own theories. He knew that time would make clear whose ideas had merit. But he worried that these departures would harm his efforts to gain acceptance for psychoanalysis. If the public saw analysts disagreeing over basic issues, they might doubt the value of Freud's work.

In a show of support, five of Freud's most loyal followers banded together in an informal group, which they called the Committee. It was the Committee's mission to assist their mentor in his work, to respond to attacks from the opponents of psycho-analysis, and to present a united front to the world.

Freud thanked his friends for their devotion. "The secret of

this Committee is that it has taken from me my most burden-some care for the future, so that I can calmly follow my path to the end," he said. He gave carved stones from his collection of antiquities to the Committee members: Sándor Ferenczi, Karl Abraham, Ernest Jones, Otto Rank, and Hanns Sachs. He told them, "You now belong to this small but select company in whose hands the future of psychoanalysis lies, and which has up to now pursued its aims in untroubled harmony." Each man had his stone set in a gold ring.

The Committee comforted Freud when Carl Jung, his Joshua, severed his ties with psychoanalysis. Jung was a strong supporter of psychoanalysis when he first visited Freud, but his thinking soon moved in another direction. Jung went on to found his own school of thought, called analytic psychology. The goal of analytic

The Committee, photographed in 1922. Standing, from left to right, are Otto Rank, Karl Abraham, Max Eitingon (who joined the select group in 1919), and Ernest Jones. Seated are Freud, Sándor Ferenczi, and Hanns Sachs.

psychology is to help the patient understand and use the contents of the unconscious to become a whole person, or fully developed "self." Jung made a distinction between the personal unconscious, which is the storage place of repressed thoughts and feelings, and the collective unconscious, which is the accumulated wisdom of the human race, gathered over many generations.

Jung said that the collective unconscious gives rise to archetypes, which are powerful symbols that have meaning throughout the world. Crosses and healing circles are examples of archetypal images. Jung, who had studied mythology and history, observed that the same story lines appear in tales from all over the world. They can be found in the myths of Greece and Rome, in the legends of Native Americans, and in the stories of the Bible. One such tale is that of the quest, in which a person leaves his or her society and travels to unknown lands in search of enlightenment. Similar characters also turn up in stories from different cultures. They include the hero of the journey, who appears, for instance, as Odysseus in Greek mythology. Modern-day scholars have pointed to Luke Skywalker in *Star Wars* as another example of the hero. Those stories and characters are archetypes, too, Jung said. They also figure in dreams, acting as guides for personal growth.

Sigmund Freud found that Jung's work lacked a scientific foundation, and he never accepted it. It was "too unintelligible, so obscured and confused that it is difficult to examine at all," he said. Nevertheless, analytic psychology has led many people to self-knowledge. Jung's ideas have been especially meaningful for artists and writers.

Psychoanalysts were not the only people disagreeing with one another. All of Europe seemed angry and defiant. Germany, Italy, and Austria-Hungary formed the Triple Alliance, promising to aid one another in case of attack. Meanwhile, Britain, France, and Russia entered into a similar agreement, the Triple Entente. Some people feared that any small disturbance might touch off a major war. After all, France had threatened war with Germany in 1905, after the Germans disputed French and Spanish control of Morocco, and Italy had declared war on Turkey in 1911.

War had nearly come to Freud's own nation in 1908, after the Austrian Empire annexed Bosnia and Herzegovina, two provinces in southern Europe. The move angered the Slavs of Serbia, who wanted to include part of Bosnia in a new Slavic nation. On June 28, 1914, a Bosnian-Serb nationalist assassinated Archduke Franz Ferdinand, the heir to the Austrian throne.

The political situation was tense in the weeks following the shooting, but the Freuds refused to believe that war was possible. They were so sure of peace that they sent eighteen-year-old Anna on a trip to England. Anna left home on July 7. Diplomatic talks broke down soon afterward, and on July 28, Austria-Hungary declared war on Serbia.

Other nations quickly chose sides and joined the conflict, which was to become the First World War. Germany backed Austria-Hungary. Russia mobilized against Austria-Hungary and Germany. France supported Russia. Sigmund and Martha held their breath when Great Britain entered the war on the Serbian, French, and Russian side. They thought of Anna constantly and worried about her safety. Would she be stuck in England for the duration of the war? Would she be imprisoned as an enemy alien? They could only hope for a swift end to the fighting.

As she approached adulthood, Anna Freud chose to pursue a life of the mind.

"I can't remember a time . . . when my horizon
was so thickly veiled by dark clouds."

CHAPTER EIGHT

Polar Night

To her parents' great relief, Anna Freud did not become a prisoner of war. British friends arranged for her to leave England with the Austrian ambassador, who had been summoned home. The Freuds waited for news of Anna's safety as she sailed with the ambassador to Gibraltar, a British colony on the Iberian Peninsula, and then to Genoa, Italy. A train carried Anna from Genoa to Vienna.

Sigmund Freud's mood was upbeat in the first months of the war. He was filled with patriotism and sure that the fighting would end quickly, with Austria victorious. He remained hopeful when two of his sons, Martin and Ernst, put themselves in the line of fire by enlisting in the army. Freud was good-natured, too, when the war broke up his inner circle. Ferenczi reported for duty as a medical officer with a unit of Hungarian hussars, or cavalry soldiers. Otto Rank was called up to serve as well.

Instead of ending quickly, though, the conflict enlarged in

scope. Turkey and Bulgaria joined the war on the side of Austria-Hungary and Germany. Together these nations were known as the Central Powers. The opposing forces—Serbia, Russia, and their partner nations—were called the Allied Powers. Before the fighting ended, twenty-two nations, including the United States, had declared war on Germany or severed relations with the German government. German forces would invade one neutral nation, Belgium.

Freud stands with his two sons in uniform,
Ernst (left) and Martin.

World War I was fought largely by foot soldiers who huddled in earthen trenches and exchanged fire with enemy forces. The lines of trenches stretched for many miles, from Switzerland to the English Channel. The German writer Erich Maria Remarque described what it was like to be a soldier in the trenches in the famous novel *All Quiet on the Western Front,* published in 1929. "The front is a cage in which we must await fearfully whatever may happen," Remarque wrote. "We lie under the network of arching shells and live in a suspense of uncertainty. Over us, Chance hovers. If a shot comes, we can duck, that is all; we neither know nor can determine where it will fall."

Shelling and sniper fire claimed millions of lives. One of the bloodiest encounters was the British assault on German positions near the Somme River in France, which occurred in the summer and fall of 1916. Britain lost more than 400,000 soldiers in the Battle of the Somme, and France lost nearly 200,000. As many as 500,000 Germans died, as well.

But even when the guns were silent, life in the trenches was brutal. Rain turned the earth to mud. Bodies littered "No Man's Land," the area between the opposing sides. Otto Dix, a German artist who fought in World War I, summed up the miserable conditions this way: "Lice, rats, barbed wire, fleas, shells, bombs, underground caves, corpses, blood, liquor, mice, cats, artillery, filth, bullets, mortars, fire, steel . . ." The soldiers wondered whether the war would ever end.

When months passed with no sign of peace, Freud's spirits dampened. The conflict that divided Europe was "the war in which we refused to believe," he said. It was bloodier and more destructive than any previous war, because progress in technology had allowed countries to create more powerful weapons. The armies of World War I were the first to use poison gas, flamethrowers, and tanks. Armored battleships were equipped with long-range guns. Submarines prowled unseen in the ocean, ready to torpedo enemy ships. The recently invented airplane became a vehicle of war, as pilots dropped bombs and showered enemy forces with machine-gun fire. The war "tramples in a blind fury on all that comes in its way, as though there were to be no future and no goodwill among men after it had passed," Freud observed.

He examined the reasons for war in a widely published essay, "Thoughts for the Time on War and Death." In this essay, Freud said that like many people, he had hoped the advances of the twentieth century would allow nations to solve their disputes without warfare. He had even dreamed that the barriers separating nations would dissolve, and that people might view the entire world as their fatherland. Once education wiped out people's warlike tendencies, the citizens of the world might enjoy "the beauty of the snow-clad mountains and of the green pasturelands; the magic of the northern forests and the splendour of the southern vegetation," Freud wrote. The world was to be a museum as well, "filled with all the treasures which the artists among civilized communities had in successive centuries created and left behind."

But his understanding of psychoanalysis told Freud that he had been fooling himself. His studies made it plain to him that "there is no such thing as *eradicating* evil tendencies." Human beings have always been born with the same instincts, including an urge to make war, he said. People suppress harmful urges in order to live in a civilized society. But, like buried memories, the basic human instincts never go away. When nations take sides in

Austrian newspapers showed their readers a glorified image of warfare, with soldiers leaping fearlessly over trenches.

a dispute and the restraints of civilization weaken, the instinct to fight and kill is no longer held in check. Freud would explore this line of thinking further in the book *Civilization and Its Discontents*, published in 1930.

Living through the war brought emotional highs and lows. It was disheartening when Russia defeated an Austrian force in one of the empire's own provinces, Galicia. But when Germany scored important victories against the Russians, people in Vienna were optimistic again.

Freud fretted about his sons now, whether the news was good or bad. Martin's unit had gone to Russia and then to Galicia. Ernst was fighting against Italy, which had broken the agreements of the Triple Alliance and joined the war on the opposing side. Studious Oliver, who had trained for an engineering career, was designing mountain tunnels and other structures for the army. Freud's worry intensified when his sister Rosa's son died in battle. And as if war casualties weren't enough, Sigmund learned that his half-brother Emanuel had been killed in a railroad accident in England. He compared the war years to a long, black night at the North Pole, where explorers waited months to see the sunrise.

The war brought hardships for all Austrians. With commerce and transportation disrupted, there was never enough fuel to provide heat in winter. Hanns Sachs described meeting with his colleagues in Freud's study, wearing "our overcoats and gloves, with our hats on our heads, suffering from the emptiness of our stomachs and frostbites on our hands." Freud often felt too cold to work. He wrote letters with numb fingers, but he put off longer writing projects until spring.

Travel was restricted, and food was rationed. Everyone learned how it felt to go hungry. The Freuds were luckier than most, thanks to Sándor Ferenczi and a friend of his from Budapest, Anton von Freund, a wealthy brewer, who smuggled bread and flour into Vienna from time to time. Another acquaintance, the grateful brother of a former patient, gave the Freuds food he obtained from Holland.

An economic depression set in, and Freud's patients dwindled in number until he saw only one or two. With almost no income, he and Martha used up their savings, and they feared bankruptcy. The psychoanalytic association stopped publishing its journals because it had no money, paper, or ink. Freud wrote to Lou Andreas-Salomé, "I do not doubt that mankind will survive even this war, but I know for certain that for me and my contemporaries the world will never again be a happy place." By the end of 1916, he had lost hope of an Austrian victory.

During this period, Freud delivered a series of Saturday lectures at the University of Vienna. Only a few people came to hear him at first, but after word got around that the talks were entertaining and informative, more and more people attended. Freud's audiences swelled to seventy, and then to one hundred.

In one lecture, Freud cautioned that it was a mistake for a young person to choose psychoanalysis for a career. "Such a choice of profession would ruin any chance he might have of success at a University," he said, "and if he started life as a practicing physician, he would find himself in a society which did not understand his efforts, which regarded him with distrust and hostility, and unleashed upon him all the evil spirits lurking within it." This talk and the others were published in two parts, in 1916 and 1917, as *Introductory Lectures on Psychoanalysis*.

There was truth in Freud's warning to the imaginary young person, and a measure of kidding, too. He very much wanted young doctors to carry on his work. He was sixty years old; he wondered how much longer he would live and whether the psychoanalytic movement would remain strong after his death. He used his time during the war to write a series of essays that summed up his thinking. It took him only a few weeks to write the first five, which dealt with instincts, repression, the unconscious, dream interpretation, and mourning and sorrow. Published in 1915, these essays are among Freud's most penetrat-

Freud's colleague
Lou Andreas-Salomé.

Shell-shocked U.S. soldiers recuperate at an American National Red Cross Hospital in the quiet forest near Blois, France.

ing works. He wrote seven more, but they were never published, and the manuscripts have been lost.

But it was World War I, more than anything else, that caused doctors to adopt psychoanalysis as a treatment method. Many soldiers who fought in the trenches suffered from an affliction known as shell shock. Constant exposure to gunfire and scenes of death brought on mental breakdown and some physical symptoms of hysteria, such as paralysis and tremors. Many shell-

shocked men complained of insomnia, while others relived the horrors of war in their dreams. Today this condition is called post-traumatic stress disorder. It occurs in survivors of painful or shocking events, including battle, crime, and abuse.

Physicians prescribed drugs for the troubled soldiers, gave them electric shock therapy, and hypnotized them, but saw little improvement. Many doctors treating shell-shocked soldiers suspected that the men were malingering—faking mental illness to escape the battlefield. These doctors were under pressure from military leaders to patch up sick and wounded men and return them to their units as soon as possible. They reasoned that if the treatment was painful enough, malingerers would prefer danger in the trenches to safety in the hospital. In some cases, therapy amounted to pure and simple cruelty. Several patients were zapped with so much electricity that they died, while others were driven to suicide. And the ones who returned to the front soon relapsed and came back to the hospital. Clearly, something new had to be tried.

Doctors on both sides of the battle lines had read about Freud's work. When they tried psychoanalysis with their patients, the outcome was encouraging. Psychiatrists who helped soldiers express the anxiety associated with war saw the men improve. Most astonishing was the fact that many cases of shell shock appeared to be linked to childhood trauma. Some doctors reported that battle conditions awakened troubling memories that had been resting in the unconscious.

By the summer of 1918, the end of the fighting was in sight. The Allies took the offensive in Europe, breaking through German lines and driving back the Central Powers. Convinced that they were losing the war, entire units of German soldiers surrendered. Many men who went home on leave never returned to the front. Beginning on August 8, some 450 Allied tanks attacked the German positions near the Somme River, and thousands of soldiers and officers surrendered.

Bulgaria signed an armistice, or cease-fire agreement, with the Allies on September 30, while the chief of the German General Staff urged his government to seek peace.

Austria-Hungary was being defeated on every battlefield, and its citizens perceived that the years of Habsburg rule were nearly over. The time had come for ethnic groups living within the empire to seize their freedom. On December 1, leaders of the Serbs, Croats, and Slovenes met in Belgrade to form a new kingdom, which became the nation of Yugoslavia. The Poles, whose land had been divided among Austrian, German, and Russian rule, were next to declare nationhood. Czechoslovakia had proclaimed its independence on October 28. Karl I, the last Habsburg emperor, renounced his right to the thrones of Austria and Hungary on November 11, the day the warring nations signed the armistice ending World War I. Austria and Hungary became independent republics, and according to the treaty signed with the Allies in 1919, there was to be no future political or economic union between Austria and Germany.

The new Austria was impoverished after the war, and public services were in disarray. The nation had lost its key industrial regions, Bohemia and Moravia, when the empire broke apart. For the Freuds and their fellow Austrians, the shortages continued. People sat down to meal after meal of watery vegetable soup. "No meat, not enough bread, no milk, potatoes and eggs extremely dear," Freud complained. He wrote to Ernest Jones, "We have grown hungry beggars all of us here." He and his family eagerly

opened packages of food sent by the relatives in England. But like the stray dogs that prowled Vienna, Freud grew thin.

The hardships didn't let up, and neither did concerns about family members in uniform. There was no word from Martin, only a rumor that his unit had been captured by the Italians. "I can't remember a time in my life when my horizon was so thickly veiled by dark clouds," Freud wrote. A letter from Martin arrived at last in December 1918, saying that he was stranded in an Italian hospital. He finally made it back to Vienna the following summer.

Sigmund and Martha had feared the loss of a son, but instead they lost a daughter. In January 1920, Sophie came down with a dangerous strain of influenza that swept through Europe and North America following World War I. She died within days. Sophie left a grieving husband and two small sons. The Freuds

Facing shortages in the aftermath of World War I, hungry people search the garbage heaps outside Vienna for anything edible.

could not even travel to their daughter's funeral or comfort her family in person. The war had disrupted railroad service between Vienna and Germany, where Sophie had lived, and the trains still were not running.

Religious people often find peace in the thought that death is a part of God's plan. Freud the atheist, however, saw no such meaning in his loss. He wrote to Sophie's husband, Max Halberstadt, "It is a senseless brutal act of fate which has taken our Sophie from us, something one cannot wrack one's brain about, a blow under which we have to bow our heads, poor helpless human beings that we are."

That same month, another senseless death occurred: Anton von Freund, the brewer who had aided the Freuds during the war, lost his life to cancer. The death of this kind friend shook Freud emotionally, making him feel older and closer to death himself.

Many people would have trouble working during such a stressful time, but not Sigmund Freud. He was as curious and productive as ever. In 1919, he started up a publishing house, the Verlag, to print books on psychoanalytical topics. He also gave thought to the basic instincts that govern human behavior.

Freud had long believed that the mind operates according to a "pleasure principle," that people choose a course of behavior to gain pleasure or at least to avoid danger, tension, or pain. Now, such an explanation seemed incomplete. It failed to account for people who fought in wars or who endangered themselves in other ways. Freud was perplexed, too, by the recurrent dreams of shell-shocked soldiers. How did reliving traumatic events in dreams jibe with his theory of wish fulfillment?

He concluded that two competing instincts govern behavior.

One, the life instinct, or Eros, is akin to the pleasure principle. This impulse makes people want to preserve their lives, protect their health, seek a mate, and reproduce. At the same time, a death instinct is at work. Because every person must die, preparing for death is one of the most important tasks facing the psyche. Freud likened this instinct to a biological urge for things to be as they were before one's life began. *"The goal of all life is death,"* he wrote, "and, casting back, *The inanimate was there before the animate."* It is the death instinct, Freud said, that leads to wars and acts of aggression.

To understand the soldiers' recurrent dreams, Freud looked to children at play. In their games, children will act out the same scenes again and again. They will also ask to hear favorite stories over and over, and they know right away if an adult uses different words or omits part of a tale. Repetition helps children master tasks and situations as they grow toward maturity. Freud suspected that a similar process was at work in the dreams of shell-shocked men, that reliving a harrowing experience in a dream is a way to master it. Thus, a dream of war could be seen as the fulfillment of a wish.

While he was resolving these issues for himself, Freud also attempted to describe the healthy human mind. He divided mental processes into three groups, which he called the id, the ego, and the superego. The id includes the most basic mental processes, those that are unconscious and immune to logical reasoning. These processes meet basic needs, such as the need for food, water, or sex. The id includes all of the energy arising from the life and death instincts. It operates without concern for society's rules and without weighing the consequences of an action. In an infant, all mental functions are id processes.

British infantry climbing a hill under shell fire to win an enemy trench. The actions of soldiers in battle and others who knowingly put their lives at risk caused Freud to theorize that a death instinct operates within the psyche.

Freud said that civilization would be impossible if the id governed all human behavior. Each person would care only about satisfying his or her own desires and would ignore the well-being of others. There would be no such thing as postponing a goal for a worthwhile purpose. People would want every need met immediately.

For this reason, according to Freud, parents and society encourage children to control the forces of the id. This is accomplished by exercising another group of mental processes, the ego, which can apply logic and foresee the results of action. The ego, which is largely conscious, emerges from the id as a child matures. It exercises self-control and solves problems. "The ego represents what we call reason and sanity, in contrast to the id, which contains the passions," Freud said. He compared the ego controlling the id to "a man on horseback, who has to hold in check the superior strength of the horse."

Another name for the third group of mental processes, the superego, is conscience. The superego monitors the actions of the ego, applying moral values and ethical rules. Freud described the superego as an unconscious inner force that determines right and wrong. In a healthy person, the id, ego, and superego operate according to a system of checks and balances. The ego is in control, yet it permits some satisfaction of desires from the id without too much chastisement from the superego.

Not everyone's mind is in proper balance, however. It seemed to Freud that a too-strong id leads to impulsive, even criminal, behavior. And an overactive superego can cripple a person with guilt. It can give rise to a morally rigid individual who is quick to pass judgment on others.

Freud described the threefold structure of the mind in another important piece of writing, *The Ego and the Id,* published in 1923. No longer did the world ignore a new book by Sigmund Freud. He had become a famous man, whose works were translated into foreign languages. The Russian version of *Introductory Lectures on Psychoanalysis* became a best-seller in the Soviet Union as soon as it was available. Pupils traveled long distances to study psychoanalysis in Vienna, and in February 1920, the Berlin Policlinic opened in Germany. It was the first facility in the world to offer psychoanalysis for patients, and research and training for analysts.

Numerous magazine articles explained Freud's ideas to the reading public. People in Europe and America added such terms as "Oedipus complex," "repression," "ego," and "id" to their vocabularies. Analysis became all the rage among the well-to-do. Hundreds of practitioners in New York called themselves psychoanalysts, whether they were qualified or not. To protect patients, the American Psychoanalytic Association restricted its membership to physicians and required analysts to compete rigorous training.

James Putnam, the neurologist who had entertained Freud in New York, marveled at the change in public opinion. He commented, "Who would have dreamed, a decade or more ago, that today college professors would be teaching Freud's doctrines to students of both sexes, scientific men turning to them for light on the nature of the instincts and educators for hints on the training of the young?"

Freudian thinking was also influencing the arts. Surrealist painters and writers stressed the role of the unconscious in creative activity. René Magritte, Salvador Dali, and others painted dreamlike scenes, hoping to connect with the unconscious minds of viewers. Authors and literary critics applied Freud's teachings to characters in novels and plays.

Some people would always reject Freud's work, though. Discussing shell shock, neurologist Silas Weir Mitchell grumbled, "Today, aided by German perplexities, we would ask the victims a hundred and twenty-one questions, consult their dreams as to why they wanted to go home, and do no better than to let them go as hopeless."

When an international psychoanalytical conference took place in the Netherlands in 1920, sixty-two representatives and fifty-seven guests attended. It cheered Freud to see scientists from once-warring nations working together again. One of those present was Anna Freud. The child who had eavesdropped on her father's meetings was now a young woman who hoped to carry on his work.

* * *

On April 20, 1923, Anna and her mother were called to a Vienna medical clinic on an urgent matter. They were shocked to find Sigmund Freud there, bleeding heavily from his jaw. Two months earlier, he had noticed a white patch inside his mouth. He had come to the clinic to have it removed, but had told no one, hoping to spare the family unnecessary concern. He expected to have a simple operation and to go home the same day, but then the hemorrhage occurred.

Anna spent the night beside her father's cot and nursed him through the crisis. The doctors at first assured Freud that the growth was nothing serious, but a biopsy confirmed what he suspected. The white patch had been cancer.

"In the Middle Ages they would have
burnt me; nowadays they are
content with burning my books."

CHAPTER NINE

Abandoning Ship

On his birthday, May 6, Sigmund Freud was already back at work. Once again he could eat normally and smoke cigars. One event clouded his happiness during the months of recovery, though. It was the death of Sophie's younger son, Heinz Rudolf, from tuberculosis. Freud spent the blackest days of his life, he said, mourning the child. It was the first time his loved ones ever saw him cry.

His mood improved in autumn, when he took Anna to Rome. "Papa wanted to show me many things and I wanted to share his seeing them again," Anna wrote to Max Eitingon. Anxiety about Freud's health prevented them from enjoying Rome as fully as they had hoped to, but they formed a closer bond as they traveled together. "I realize . . . for the first time what good company my little daughter is," Freud confided to Lou Andreas-Salomé.

Anna helped her father cope with bleeding from his mouth that occurred suddenly while they were away from home. And she nursed him following a second operation for cancer in late

October 1923. This complicated surgery lasted seven hours. The physician, one of Europe's leading oral surgeons, slit open Freud's lip and cheek to remove the right half of his upper jaw and palate. The procedure was so tricky that the doctor practiced first on a cadaver to be sure he could do it.

The surgery left a gaping hole in the roof of Freud's mouth. He was fitted with a medical device to separate his oral and nasal cavities. Freud hated the awkward metal contraption, which he nicknamed "the Monster." Even with the prosthesis in place, he ate and spoke with difficulty.

Freud needed a third, smaller operation on November 17, to remove additional cancer. He would have surgery more than thirty times over the next thirteen years, as doctors cut away pre-cancerous tissue from his mouth. He lived with constant pain but rarely complained. "It is no use quarreling with fate," he liked to say. He refused painkillers, fearing they would dull his thinking. Still, he knew a time might come when he was in great pain and near death. He made his doctor promise that if that day ever arrived, he would receive a heavy dose of medication—enough, possibly, to end his life. Freud did not want to suffer needlessly.

The founder of psychoanalysis disliked appearing in public now, so when an international meeting of analysts took place in Salzburg, Austria, in April 1924, Anna attended in his place. More and more, Anna acted as Freud's representative, but she did not just work in her father's shadow. She was distinguishing herself as a psychologist specializing in disturbances in children. Soon, she replaced Otto Rank on the Committee.

In 1923, Rank had published *The Trauma of Birth*, a book outlining his own theory of psychological development. Rank claimed that the experience of birth, with the shock of moving

from the womb to the outer world, triggers all of life's anxieties. Freud had trouble accepting Rank's ideas, but he urged the Committee members to support one another's work for the good of psychoanalysis. "Complete agreement, in all detailed questions of science and its newly opened problems is not possible among half a dozen men of different personality, and it is not even desirable," he remarked.

Karl Abraham thought that Freud was being too soft, and pressured him to speak up. If Freud thought that Rank's theory was nonsense, he should say so, Abraham prodded. As it turned out, Freud's reaction hardly mattered. Otto Rank severed his ties with Vienna, moved to New York, and became one of the best-known analysts in the United States.

Freud felt surer of himself in criticizing his old friend Ferenczi when he devised a new treatment approach. Ferenczi had decided that neurotic patients suffer most from a lack of love in

Anna and Sigmund Freud in 1928. Anna Freud is remembered for her work in the psychoanalysis of children. She founded the Hampstead Child Therapy Clinic in London in 1947.

childhood. It was therefore important for analysts to supply that missing love, to embrace patients and shower them with affection. He also insisted that therapy be brief, lasting a few months at most.

Freud foresaw danger in expressions of affection between analysts and patients. It was too easy for embraces to lead to kisses and other acts, he warned Ferenczi. He believed that a detached, objective approach worked best. And as for rapid treatment, Freud gently explained that real progress takes time. "In my recent illness I learned that a shaved beard takes six weeks to grow again," he said. "Three months have passed since my last operation, and I am still suffering from the changes in the scar tissue. So I find it hard to believe that in only a slightly longer time . . . one can penetrate to the deepest layers of the unconscious and bring about lasting changes in the mind." Freud and Ferenczi remained cordial after this frank talk, but they were never again as close as they once had been.

A new friend entered Freud's circle in 1925. Marie Bonaparte was French and a distant niece of Napoleon. She had wanted to be a doctor when she was young, but her family had discouraged scientific ambition in a girl. She grew up to become a princess instead of a doctor, marrying Prince George of Greece. After coming to Vienna to be analyzed by Freud, Bonaparte studied psychoanalysis and founded an institute in Paris.

In 1926, Freud turned seventy. He received birthday cards and telegrams from people all over the world. Much of the praise embarrassed him, but he was pleased with some of the tributes, such as the one from his brothers in B'nai B'rith. Freud thanked the men for their friendship over the years, saying in a letter, "At a time when no one in Europe would listen to me and I had no pupils in Vienna, you offered me your sympathetic attention. You were my first audience."

One birthday message came from Albert Einstein. The Freuds met the great physicist and his wife a few months later, in December 1926. Sigmund Freud found Einstein to be "cheerful, sure of himself and agreeable." He quipped that Einstein "understands as much about psychology as I do about physics, so we had a very pleasant talk."

For many years now, Freud had been sure that the end of his life was near. At seventy, he announced that he was ready to retire, and he dissolved the Committee. But the mind of Sigmund Freud was too active for retirement. He recently had published his autobiography, and he still saw three patients a day.

Marie Bonaparte (left) and her daughter, Princess Eugenie.

He now refined his description of the ego and examined the ways it defends itself against feelings or impulses that it cannot accept. He noted that we all have a dark side consisting of personality traits and feelings that we are unprepared to face. He described the defense mechanisms that the ego might employ to keep those impulses out of the conscious mind. For example, a common defense mechanism is denial: It occurs when someone fails to see or acknowledge an unpleasant truth. In another defense mechanism, rationalization, a person finds a worthy motive for behavior that really occurs for a less commendable reason.

Freud derived great pleasure from spending time with his grandchildren. Here he holds Oliver's daughter, Eva, as Eva's mother, Henny Fuchs Freud, looks on.

Sigmund Freud never stopped expanding his interests, even in old age. He learned to love animals, something he had never had time for when he was younger. He made friends with Anna's German shepherd, Wolf. In fact, he doted on the dog, feeding Wolf table scraps and turning on lights for him when the room grew dim. The rest of the family found this hilarious and asked Freud whether Wolf wanted to read. In 1928, a friend of Anna's gave Freud a dog of his own, a chow named Lun Yu. He was heart-broken when Lun Yu, just fifteen months old, broke free from her leash and was struck by a train. His next chow, Jofi, was a loyal companion who snoozed at Freud's feet during his sessions with patients. "When Jofi got up and yawned, the time was up," Martin Freud remembered. "She was never late in announcing the end of a session."

The year 1930 brought both loss and recognition to the Freud household. Sigmund's mother, Amalia Freud, died that year at the age of ninety-five. Although Freud and his mother had always

The sons of Ernst Freud: Stephan, Klemens, and Lucian. Lucian Freud grew up to become an accomplished artist.

Amalia Freud remained a beautiful woman late in life and still took pains to dress well.

been close, he confessed to Sándor Ferenczi that his reaction to her death was a strange one. "No pain, no grief, which probably can be explained by the special circumstances—her great age, my pity for her helplessness toward the end." Another part of his reaction was relief. He had feared he might die before his mother did.

In 1930, Freud was awarded the Goethe Prize, named for the author credited with writing "Nature," the essay that had inspired him so many years earlier. The city of Frankfurt, Germany, presents the prestigious literary prize in memory of its most famous resident. Freud said that honors like this one would have meant much to him when he was young, but in later life they were "threatening calamities" that disturbed the order of his days. Anna traveled to Frankfurt to accept the award for him. She also journeyed to Freiberg when the citizens of that little town hung a plaque on the house where Freud was born.

People who live a long time often see history repeat itself, and Sigmund Freud had that experience. Anti-Semitism was surfacing in Austria and in other countries, as it had when he was young. This time, though, the hatred of Jews was more ominous.

Many Jews had migrated to Vienna from surrounding regions after World War I. The city had absorbed the influx until 1929, when the American stock market crash affected economies throughout the world. The principal Austrian bank, the Kreditanstalt, nearly collapsed in 1931, and many people lost their savings. Businesses failed, and before long, one-third of Austrian workers were unemployed. Many people spoke out openly against the Jews, claiming that they were competing unfairly for jobs. The voters elected a strongly Catholic, anti-Jewish government.

The situation was worse in Germany, where the National Socialist Party—the Nazis—took control of the government in 1933. Following orders from their dictator, Adolf Hitler, the Nazis set out to reorganize society, to rid Germany of anyone not of "Aryan," or "pure German," stock. The police had the authority to arrest any person and commit him or her to a concentration camp. The list of "undesirables" targeted for arrest was a long one that included Communists, Gypsies, homosexuals, Jehovah's Witnesses, political dissenters, prostitutes, and, of course, Jews.

Anna Freud spoke on behalf of her father in 1931, when the people of Freiberg unveiled a plaque marking his birthplace.

Hitler's government stripped Jews of responsibility in society and denied them credit for their achievements. Because Freud and many of his colleagues were Jews, the Nazis denounced "Jewish psychoanalysis." They disbanded the German Psychoanalytical Society and replaced it with the International General Medical Society for Psychotherapy. The head of this new, Nazi-sanctioned organization was Carl Jung, Freud's former protégé. Jung's group studied Adolf Hitler's book, *Mein Kampf* (My Struggle), and tried to separate Jewish from Aryan contributions to the study of the mind. Germany took a bolder step in May 1933, when five thousand students wearing swastikas threw books by Freud and other Jewish thinkers into a bonfire. Freud joked darkly, "What progress we are making! In the Middle Ages they would have burnt me; nowadays they are content with burning my books."

Friends, warning that Hitler planned to expand his power, begged Freud to flee. If Hitler's Germany took over Austria, Freud would be in danger. Already, the Nazis had seized all property in the German offices of the Verlag, the psychoanalytical book publisher. Go to Switzerland, England, or even South America, the friends pleaded. But Freud would hear none of it. Vienna was his lifelong home. Besides, he insisted, Austria was safe from German occupation. The Treaty of St. Germain forbade such an alliance. And although there were Nazis living in Austria, he was sure they would never be as cruel as the German party members.

He turned his attention to the past, to the history of the Jewish people. He immersed himself in the story of Moses, the great prophet and leader, hoping to discover why Jews had been persecuted through the centuries.

Time seems to pass more quickly as life progresses. Already it

Freud at work, accompanied by his beloved Jofi.

was 1936, and Freud was turning eighty. Once more, greetings poured in from around the world. Freud heard from Einstein and from the German writer Hermann Hesse, who said that Freud's theories had influenced his fiction. Visitors called at 19 Berggasse all day. When one well-wisher asked how he was feeling, Freud replied, "How a man of eighty feels is not a topic of conversation." At eighty, Freud was admitted to the Royal Society. This elite scientific body, headquartered in London, was founded in 1660.

Two months after his birthday, Freud went to the hospital for surgery on his mouth. He had had many operations to treat precancerous lesions, but he had been cancer-free for thirteen years.

Freud poses for sculptor
Oscar Némon, 1937.

This time, the surgeons found cancer. They removed it and warned that another tumor could appear at any time.

The cancer was not the only sign that life as Sigmund Freud had known it would never be the same. On March 11, 1938, German forces entered Austria without opposition. On March 12, Nazi tanks patrolled the streets of Vienna. Freud wrote in his journal, "Finis Austriae"—"The End of Austria."

Several Nazis appeared at 19 Berggasse the very next day. They left after Anna Freud paid them off with 6,000 Austrian schillings, but they threatened to come back. Meanwhile, a mob broke into the Vienna office of the Verlag, which was under the direction of Martin Freud.

Other Jews received harsher treatment. Nazis—both German and Austrian—forced Jewish men, women, and children to scrub the city streets with toothbrushes. Nazi storm troopers and Hitler Youth heckled the terrified people, while the cleaning solution of water and acid burned their fingers. In the holy season of Passover, Jews were dragged into the city parks, thrown to the ground, and made to eat grass as if they were cattle or sheep. Nazis mistook another old man named Freud for the famous psychoanalyst and attacked him on the street. Fortunately, he survived.

Ernest Jones and Marie Bonaparte came to occupied Vienna and urged Freud to get out. The aging doctor balked, claiming that he was too frail to make the trip. Jones, who was a physician, pronounced him well enough to travel. Freud then said that no country would take him in, and Jones admitted that he had a point. Nations grappling with economic depression were reluctant to admit refugees who might take jobs away from their citizens. But Jones had a hunch that England would make an exception for such a famous person as Sigmund Freud.

Finally Freud argued that leaving Vienna would be like deserting a sinking ship. Jones now made him see that the ship had already deserted him. The Vienna he knew and loved no longer existed, and his friends were gone. Max Eitingon had immigrated to Palestine. Hanns Sachs had settled in Boston, while Jones was living in England. Karl Abraham and Sándor Ferenczi had died recently, and so had Jofi. Freud reluctantly agreed that the wisest course for himself and his family was to leave.

A relieved Ernest Jones returned to England to arrange for

Jews are forced to clean the streets of Vienna prior to Hitler's arrival.

the Freuds' arrival. It would take time to secure exit visas from Austrian authorities and permission from the British government for the Freuds to enter the country. Marie Bonaparte stayed in Vienna. She hoped that her status as a member of a royal family might offer the Freuds some protection. But her daily visits didn't stop the Nazis from returning to 19 Berggasse.

Several men from the Gestapo—Hitler's ruthless secret police—arrived on the morning of March 22. Armed with guns, they brazenly searched cupboards and drawers for anti-Nazi material. The frightened family watched in silence as uniformed men rifled their home. When one of the troopers threw her neatly folded table linens on the floor, however, Martha Freud protested. She gave the intruders a tongue-lashing, and they left her household goods alone.

The Nazis found no incriminating papers, but they took Anna Freud in for questioning anyway. Anna's face betrayed no fear as she rode off with her captors; her father, though, was sick with worry for her safety. He chain-smoked cigars, although he was not supposed to smoke anymore, and he paced up and down. As a boy, he had vowed to fight anti-Semitism. But as an old man facing hatred in its most virulent form, he was powerless. He cried tears of joy when Anna returned at night unharmed. He never knew that she secretly had carried a capsule of poison to Gestapo headquarters. Anna had planned to kill herself rather than submit to torture or imprisonment in a concentration camp.

By May, all the needed visas and letters of permission were at last in order. It was time to go. Leaving meant saying good-bye forever to four of Freud's sisters, who were to remain in Vienna. (His sister Anna lived in New York.) The family crossed their fingers in the hope that the old women would be safe from Nazi harass-

ment. Leaving also meant closing the door to the office where, for more than thirty-five years, Freud had treated patients from all over the world.

Minna Bernays was in failing health and so was the first to leave. Anna's American-born friend Dorothy Burlingham escorted Aunt Minna to London on May 5. Martin's family departed on May 14, and Mathilde's left ten days later. Ernst was already in London, and Oliver had been living in France since 1933. Alexander Freud, Sigmund's brother, was safe in Switzerland.

Sigmund, Martha, Anna, two servants, Freud's physician, and his new dog, Lun, boarded a train for Paris on June 4. They got out of Vienna none too soon. In the previous month alone, two thousand Viennese Jews had been sent to Dachau, a concentration camp near Munich, Germany.

Austrian citizens are made to salute as German police enter the town of Imst in March 1938.

"... I have made many beginnings and thrown out many suggestions."

CHAPTER TEN

"The Patchwork of Life's Labours"

Marie Bonaparte and her husband, Prince George, met the travelers at the Paris railroad station. Ernst Freud was there, too, and so was Harry Freud, the son of Sigmund's brother, Alexander. After spending an afternoon with the princess and prince, the Freuds boarded a night ferry to Dover, on England's southern coast. As he crossed the English Channel in darkness, Freud thought about the military heroes he had admired as a child. He dozed and dreamed that he was tracing the route of William the Conqueror, who took an army from France to England in 1066. After defeating the British at the Battle of Hastings, William crowned himself king of England.

Freud felt like a conquering king when he reached London on June 6. The English people welcomed his family warmly. Friends and strangers alike sent flowers and greetings, and Anna spent many hours replying to letters and telegrams. Shopkeepers and cabbies recognized Freud from his photographs in newspapers, while Britain's leading medical journal, *The Lancet*, evaluated Freud's impact on his profession. "His teachings have in their time aroused controversy more acute and antagonism more bitter than any since the days of Darwin," the editors stated. "Now, in his old age, there are few psychologists of any school who do not admit their debt to him." Freud remarked, "For the first time and late in life I have experienced what it is to be famous."

Anna Freud spoke publicly on her family's behalf. She said that the Freuds had been treated well in Vienna, and that everyone in that city, from police officers to government officials, "have

The Freuds rest at the Paris home of Marie Bonaparte before resuming their journey. Left to right: Anna, Sigmund, the chow Lun, Martha, and Ernst.

been very friendly to us." Anna made that statement with the safety of loved ones in mind. The family feared that the Nazis might take revenge on their relatives in Austria if they spoke truthfully about their treatment.

Freud had many callers in London, both famous people and old friends. The science fiction writer H. G. Wells visited him, and so did the Spanish surrealist painter Salvador Dali, who sketched him. Freud chatted with the granddaughter of Josef Breuer, the doctor with whom he had written *Studies on Hysteria* in the 1890s. Before leaving Vienna, Freud had used his connections to help Breuer's widow escape from Austria, and the granddaughter wanted to thank him. One momentous afternoon, the secretaries of the Royal Society brought the group's Charter Book for Freud to sign. It delighted the aged psychoanalyst to write his name in the same book that contained the signatures of Isaac Newton, Charles Darwin, and other great scientists.

When there were no visitors, Freud kept busy arranging his study. A former servant in Vienna had shipped his books and antiquities to him, and they had arrived undamaged. He also took pleasure in the flower garden outside his new home, but it saddened him to think that age and illness would prevent him from enjoying it much longer. He saw a small number of patients now, and he continued to write. He was finishing his last book, *Moses and Monotheism,* a meditation on the history of the Jewish people that was published in 1938.

Once more, a book by Freud was criticized, but not because people had trouble accepting his theories of the mind. Jewish scholars denounced *Moses and Monotheism* because Freud put forth the idea that Moses had been an Egyptian by birth, and not an Israelite. There was no historical documentation to support that notion, they said, adding that Freud was delving into areas where he lacked expertise. Other readers simply thought that *Moses and Monotheism* was not one of Freud's best works. Freud himself came to regret publishing a book that could be viewed as critical of Jews at a time when the Jewish people were being persecuted as never before.

The Nazis had stepped up their effort to eliminate Jews from public life in the regions under their control. The events of a single night in 1938 encapsulated all the hate and danger that the Jews faced under National Socialism. On that night, Hitler's forces burned hundreds of synagogues in Germany, smashed the windows of Jewish-owned businesses, arrested Jewish shop owners, and set fire to Jews' homes. The world remembers November 9, 1938, as Kristallnacht, the Night of Broken Glass.

As he read newspaper accounts of Nazi terrorism, Freud was recovering from another operation on his jaw. This surgery had lasted more than two hours. It had left him with many stitches in his cheek and lip and a weakened body. He needed another operation a month later. Then, in February 1939, his doctors noticed an odd swelling in his mouth. They called in one of the world's top cancer experts, who confirmed what the medical team suspected: Freud's cancer had spread, and science could do nothing for him now.

Freud knew that his life would soon end. He spent his final months on the ground floor of his home, close to the garden. He saw some patients and worked on a book, *An Outline of Psychoanalysis*, which he would never finish. He fol-

Freud's London home. Today it houses the Sigmund Freud Museum.

Freud labors to finish his final book, MOSES AND MONOTHEISM.

lowed the news from Europe, learning in March 1939 that Hitler had acquired all of Czechoslovakia and was threatening Poland. Freud understood that Hitler would bring war to Europe, and he predicted that the coming war would mean the defeat of Nazism.

Freud managed to work productively through most of the summer, but each day required more effort than the one before it. On August 12, his nephew Harry came to see him. Harry was going to travel across the Atlantic Ocean and would not be in England again until late December. "You won't see me here when you return," Freud said to the young man.

By September 21, Freud's pain was so great that he could no longer work or enjoy the company of family and friends. He reminded his doctor, Max Schur, of a promise he had made years earlier, when he had become Freud's physician. "Now it's nothing but torture and makes no sense any more," Freud said. Schur understood that Freud wanted to end his suffering. He gave his patient a shot of morphine that eased the pain and allowed him to sleep. After a second dose of morphine, Freud slipped into a coma.

On the evening of September 23, Anna Freud Bernays turned on a radio in New York, where she had raised five children, and learned that her older brother had died. The news caused her to remember Sigmund Freud in childhood, and to reflect on the fact that her adopted country had embraced Freud's ideas before his native land did. "America saw my brother's greatness while Europe's politics have blinded it. His discoveries owe a debt to America, one that my descendants will help to repay," she vowed.

Psychoanalysts and scientists tried to sum up Freud's importance. "Before he came on the scene no one understood the underlying factors of abnormal behavior. Psychiatry was barren and uninteresting. The best achievements of his predecessors . . . told us nothing concerning the dynamic factors at the bottom of the neuroses and psychoses," commented the psychiatrist Abraham Brill, who translated many of Freud's writings into English. "His works are studied wherever there is any civilization."

"There is every reason to think that one hundred years hence Freud will be classified with Copernicus and Newton as one of the men who opened up new vistas of thought," said Dr. Winfred Overholser of Washington, D.C. Another writer pointed out that every scientific breakthrough requires an instrument of research. For example, "the microscope [revealed] the mystery of ultimate bodily structure and the existence of microbes," he

stated. Freud's instrument of research, the writer said, was free association.

The poet W. H. Auden concluded about Freud, "All he did was to remember / like the old and be honest like children."

Freud's body was cremated and, as he had wished, his ashes were placed in a Grecian urn from his collection. The military conflict that he had prophesied for Europe had begun just weeks before his death. He did not live to see the Allied victory in World War II and the defeat of Hitler. He never knew that his four aging sisters in Vienna died in Nazi concentration camps.

The people who knew Freud well praised his character. His old friend Ernest Jones recalled a letter Freud had written many years earlier. Freud was writing about ethics, and in his letter he remarked, "I have in fact never done anything mean." Jones asked, "How many of us, if we search our hearts, could truthfully say that?"

One of the simplest and most moving tributes came from Martha Freud, who had lived a long and useful life out of the public eye. Martha wrote to an old friend, "How terribly difficult it is to have to do without him. To continue to live without so much kindness and wisdom beside one! It is small comfort for me to know that in the fifty-three years of our married life not one angry word fell between us."

People are likely to be evaluating Freud's work well into the twenty-first century, and perhaps beyond. Whether the bulk of his ideas fall in or out of favor, he made some contributions of lasting value. Psychoanalysis and dream interpretation remain effective aids for studying the unconscious. While medication can often provide swift remedies for psychological ills, analysis remains a better tool for improving self-understanding. Freud

"I have never ceased my analytic work nor my writing." Sigmund Freud at the end of a full life.

also demonstrated to the world that unconscious motives govern human behavior. He made people aware of the psychological lives of children and changed the attitudes of countless parents and teachers. He has had a profound influence on the arts, affecting such creative endeavors as the depiction of characters in novels and the use of imagery in painting.

In 1925, as his seventieth birthday neared, Freud reflected on his long career. "Looking back, then, over the patchwork of my life's labours, I can say that I have made many beginnings and thrown out many suggestions," he wrote. "Something will come of them in the future, though I cannot tell myself whether it will be much or little. I can, however, express a hope that I have opened up a pathway for an important advance in our knowledge."

ENDNOTES

CHAPTER ONE
WRESTLING DEMONS

Freud, "Say whatever goes through your mind'" is quoted in Ernest Jones, *The Life and Work of Sigmund Freud* (New York: Basic Books, 1961), p. 145.

Freud, "the ramparts of a palace . . ." is from Sigmund Freud, "The Aetiology of Hysteria," in *The Standard Edition of the Complete Psychological Works of Sigmund Freud*. James Strachey, general editor (vol. III, London: Hogarth Press and the Institute of Psycho-Analysis, 1962), p. 191.

Freud, "One gets the impression . . ." is quoted in Jones, 1961, p. 179.

"Scientific fairy tale" is quoted in Jones, 1961, p. 171.

"Jewish swindle" is quoted in Jonathan Miller, ed., *Freud: The Man, His World, His Influence* (Boston: Little, Brown, 1972), p. 10.

"This is not a topic for discussion . . ." is quoted in Jones, 1961, p. 299.

Freud, "What is new . . ." is from Sigmund Freud, *Dora: An Analysis of a Case of Hysteria* (New York: Collier Books, 1963 [1963a]), p. 26.

"I was used to seeing patients' personalities . . ." is from Peter D. Kramer, *Listening to Prozac: A Psychiatrist Explores Antidepressant Drugs and the Remaking of the Self* (New York: Viking, 1993), pp. xiv–xv.

Freud, "Let the biologists go . . ." is quoted in C. P. Oberndorf, *A History of Psychoanalysis in America* (New York: Grune and Stratton, 1953), p. 158.

Freud, "No one who, like me . . ." is from *Sigmund Freud: An Autobiographical Study* (New York: W. W. Norton and Co. 1963 [1963b]), p. 131.

CHAPTER TWO
FAVORITE SON

Freud, "Such prophecies must be made . . ." is from Sigmund Freud, *The Major Works of Sigmund Freud*. William Benton, publisher (Chicago: Encyclopaedia Britannica, 1952), p. 216.

Freud, "If a man has been . . ." is from Sigmund Freud, "A Childhood Recollection from *Dichtung und Wahreit*," in *The Standard Edition . . .* (vol. XVII, 1955), p. 156.

Freud, "that prehistoric old woman" is quoted in Jones, 1961, p. 6.

"Fallen Ones of March" is from William M. Johnston, *Vienna, Vienna: The Golden Age, 1815–1914* (New York: Clarkson N. Potter, 1980), p. 29.

Freud, "always expecting something . . ." is quoted in Jones, 1961, p. 4.

Anna Freud (sister), "Sigi was greatly impressed . . ." is from Anna Freud Bernays, "My Brother, Sigmund Freud," *American Mercury,* November 1940, p. 338.

"Jew, get off the pavement!" is quoted in Freud, 1952, p. 218. The rest of the story is also from this source.

Freud, "We became friends . . ." is quoted in Ernst Freud, Lucie Freud, and Ilse Grumbrich-Simitis, eds., *Sigmund Freud: His Life in Pictures and Words* (New York: W. W. Norton, 1978), p. 67.

Freud, "We shared our frugal suppers . . ." is quoted in Ernst Freud et al., p. 67.

"Nature! We are surrounded . . ." is quoted in T. H. Huxley, "Nature! Aphorisms by Goethe," *Nature,* November 4, 1869, p. 9.

Freud, "I shall gain insight . . ." is quoted in Ronald W. Clark, *Freud: The Man and the Cause* (New York: Random House, 1980), p. 28.

"Eighth wonder of the world" and "an enormous cake" are quoted in Johnston, p. 135.

"Interesting, but it didn't bowl me over" and Freud's other comments on the exhibition are quoted in Ernst Freud et al., pp. 4 and 5.

"Masters over the World" is quoted in George E. Berkley, *Vienna and Its Jews: The Tragedy of Success, 1880s–1980s* (Lanham, Md.: Madison Books, 1988), p. 71.

CHAPTER THREE
BECOMING A DOCTOR

Freud, "I found that I was expected . . ." is from Freud, 1963b, p. 14.

Freud, "I put up, without much regret . . ." is from Freud, 1963b, p. 15.

Freud, "Perhaps, dear friend . . ." is quoted in Clark, p. 38.

Freud, "restrict some of the evils . . ." is quoted in Clark, p. 38.

Freud, "an Englishman in every sense . . ." is quoted in Clark, p. 37.

Emanuel Freud, "You have given us great pleasure . . ." is quoted in Bernays, p. 340.

Freud, "What he said to me was brief . . ." is from Freud, 1952, p. 304.

Anna Freud (sister), "One would have imagined . . ." is from Bernays, p. 340.

Freud, "habit of research" is quoted in Ernst Freud et al., p. 13.

Freud, "religious prejudices" is quoted in Jones, 1961, p. 81.

Freud, "I observe that I do not gain . . ." is quoted in Jones, 1961, p. 84.

Freud, "One is very crazy . . ." is quoted in Jones, 1961, p. 87.

"Whoever needs more than five hours . . ." is quoted in Clark, p. 54.

Freud, "And would you believe . . ." is quoted in Ernst Freud et al., p. 14.

"The limit of safety . . ." is from "Accidents from the Electric Current," *American Journal of Insanity,* July 1892, p. 79.

Freud, "I have really become a doctor" is quoted in Jones, 1961, p. 46.

CHAPTER FOUR
WORKING, HOPING, RISKING

Freud, "a little home . . ." is from Ernst L. Freud, ed., *The Letters of Sigmund Freud* (New York: Basic Books, 1960), p. 71.

Freud, "Strange creatures are billeted . . ." is from Ernst L. Freud, p. 15.

Freud, "I am very stubborn . . ." is quoted in Clark, p. 38.

Freud, "Before I met you . . ." is quoted in Clark, p. 38.

Brücke, "Dr. Freud is a man . . ." is quoted in Siegfried Bernfield, "Sigmund Freud, M.D.: 1882–1885," *International Journal of Psychoanalysis,* July 1951, p. 215.

Freud, "When I come I am going to . . ." is from Ernst L. Freud, p. 167.

Freud, "He used to look again and again . . ." is quoted in Ernst Freud et al., p. 117.

Freud, "whose personality and whose work . . ." is quoted in Jones, 1961, p. 145.

Freud, "but how this Sarah can act . . ." is from Ernst L. Freud, p. 180.

Freud, "Assyrian kings—tall as trees . . ." is from Ernst L. Freud, p. 173.

Freud, "had no more relation to reality . . ." is from Freud, 1952, p. 27.

Freud, "we would need two or three little rooms . . ." is from Ernst L. Freud, p. 27.

"My dear sir . . ." is quoted in Freud, 1952, p. 26.

Freud, "I am far from thinking . . ." is quoted in Ernst Freud et al., p. 124.

Freud, "She has already grown . . ." is quoted in Peter Gay, *Freud: A Life for Our Time* (New York: W. W. Norton, 1988), p. 54.

Freud, "powerful mental processes . . ." is from Freud, 1952, p. 30.

CHAPTER FIVE
THE TALKING CURE

Freud, "When our little Mathilde chuckles . . ." is quoted in Ernst Freud et al., p. 124.

Breuer, "frightening hallucinations . . ." is from Sigmund Freud and Josef Breuer, *Studies on Hysteria*, in *The Standard Edition . . .* (vol. II, 1955), p. 24.

Breuer, "She asked for something to drink . . ." is from Freud and Breuer, p. 34.

Anna O., "the talking cure" is quoted in Freud and Breuer, p. 30.

Freud, "It was only a question . . ." is from Freud and Breuer, p. 110.

Freud, "How long have you had . . ." is from Freud and Breuer, p. 110.

Freud, "I placed my hand . . ." is from Freud and Breuer, p. 110.

Breuer, "Freud's intellect is soaring . . ." is quoted in Gerard Lauzun, *Sigmund Freud: The Man and His Theories* (Greenwich, Conn.: Fawcett Books, 1962), p. 42.

Freud and Breuer, "Any experience which calls up . . ." is from Freud and Breuer, p. 6.

Freud and Breuer, "Hysterics suffer mainly . . ." is from Freud and Breuer, p. 7.

"That it may one day become possible . . ." is quoted in Jones, 1961, p. 165.

Freud, "I have the distinct feeling . . ." is quoted in Clark, p. 117.

"In those days, when one mentioned . . ." is from Max Graf, "Reminiscences of Professor Sigmund Freud," *Psychoanalytic Quarterly,* October 1942, p. 469.

Freud, "splendid isolation" is quoted in Jones, 1961, p. 239.

Freud, "I hope to be occupied . . ." is quoted in Ernst Freud et al., p. 147.

Freud, "the most important event . . ." is from Freud, 1952, p. 18.

Freud, "His life had been over . . ." is from Ernst L. Freud, p. 232.

Freud, "days when I slink about . . ." is quoted in Jones, 1961, p. 214.

Freud, "The Greek myth seizes . . ." is quoted in Clark, p. 167.

Freud, "to direct our first sexual impulses . . ." is from Freud, 1952, p. 247.

CHAPTER SIX
THE "ROYAL ROAD"

Freud, "This first account . . ." is from Freud, 1963a, p. 30.

Freud, "I have such unruly dreams" is quoted in Clark, p. 174.

Freud, "The dream is not meaningless . . ." is from Freud, 1952, p. 189.

Freud, "If you still have pains . . ." is from Freud, 1952, p. 182.

Freud, "The dream represents a certain state . . ." is from Freud, 1952, p. 188.

Martin Freud, "It was unusual for him . . ." is from Martin Freud, *Sigmund Freud: Man and Father* (New York: Jason Aronson, 1983), p. 67.

Freud, "to a knowledge of the unconscious . . ." is from Freud, 1952, p. 381.

Freud, "Insight such as this . . ." is from Freud, 1952, p. 135.

Freud, "the starting point of a new . . ." is from Freud, 1963b, p. 90.

Freud, "Here the secret of dreams . . ." is quoted in Jones, 1961, p. 230.

Freud, "Even dreams with a painful content . . ." is from Freud, 1952, p. 204.

Freud, "everyone has wishes . . ." is from Freud, 1952, p. 204.

Freud, "The most complex mental operations . . ." is from Freud, 1952, p. 375.

Graf, "Freud was that queer fellow . . ." is from Graf, p. 469.

Freud, "They may abuse my doctrines by day . . ." is quoted in Ernest Jones, *Sigmund Freud: Four Centenary Addresses* (New York: Basic Books, 1956), p. 46.

Freud, "The time is not ripe . . ." is from Marie Bonaparte, Anna Freud, and Ernst Kris, eds., *The Origins of Psychoanalysis: Letters to Wilhelm Fliess, Drafts and Notes, 1887–1902, by Sigmund Freud* (London: Imago, 1954), p. 304.

Anna Freud (daughter), "even tempered, optimistic . . ." is quoted in Gay, p. 159.

Martin Freud, "He would run to it . . ." is from Martin Freud, p. 59.

Freud, "The things put me in high spirits . . ." is quoted in Gay, p. 172.

Freud, "What a pity one can't live here always!" is from Ernst L. Freud, p. 266.

Freud, "science of unconscious mental processes" is from Sigmund Freud, "Psychoanalysis," in Clifton Fadiman, ed., *The Treasury of the Encyclopaedia Britannica* (New York: Viking Penguin, 1992), p. 413.

Freud, "In every instance the treatment makes heavy claims . . ." is from Fadi-
   man, pp. 413–14.
Freud, "If you attack the symptom . . ." is quoted in Hanns Sachs, *Freud: Master
   and Friend* (Cambridge, Mass.: Harvard University Press, 1944), p. 45.
Adler, "This man has something to say . . ." is quoted in Phyllis Bottome, *Alfred
   Adler: Apostle of Freedom* (London: Faber and Faber, 1939), p. 69.
Stekel, "We were like pioneers . . ." is from Emil A. Gutheil, ed., *The Autobiography
   of Wilhelm Stekel: The Life Story of a Pioneer Psychoanalyst* (New York:
   Liveright, 1950), p. 116.
Freud, "had officially recognized the role . . ." is quoted in Jones, 1961, p. 222.

CHAPTER SEVEN
PROPHET

Freud, "have a meaning . . ." is from Freud, 1952, p. 4.
Freud, "repressed wishes . . ." is from Freud, 1952, p. 4.
Jung, "Freud was the first man . . ." is from Carl G. Jung, *Memories, Dreams,
   Reflections* (London: Collins, Routledge and Kegan Paul, 1963), p. 149.
Freud, "son and heir" is quoted in Jones, 1961, p. 253.
Freud, "If I am Moses . . ." is from William McGuire, ed., *The Freud/Jung Letters:
   The Correspondence Between Sigmund Freud and C. G. Jung* (Princeton, N.J.:
   Princeton University Press, 1974), pp. 125–26.
Freud, "to bear witness that all the opposition . . ." is from Ernst L. Freud,
   p. 254.
Martin Freud, "We were never ordered . . ." is quoted in Gay, p. 161.
Freud, "In Europe I felt as though I were despised . . ." is from Freud, 1963b,
   p. 99.
Freud, "Now hystericals and all neurotics . . ." is from Freud, 1952, p. 4.
Freud, "America is a mistake . . ." is quoted in Jones, 1961, p. 270.
Freud, "the beginnings of religion . . ." is from Sigmund Freud, *Totem and Taboo
   and Other Works,* in *The Standard Edition . . .* (vol. XIII, 1960), p. 156.
Freud, "I can only say that I encountered . . ." is quoted in Clark, p. 299.
Freud, "The secret of this Committee . . ." is quoted in Ernst Freud et al.,
   p. 200.
Freud, "You now belong to this small but select . . ." is quoted in Ernst Freud et
   al., p. 200.
Freud, "too unintelligible, so obscured . . ." is quoted in Lauzun, p. 69.

CHAPTER EIGHT
POLAR NIGHT

"The front is a cage . . ." is from Erich Maria Remarque, *All Quiet on the Western
   Front* (New York: Fawcett Crest, 1982), p. 101.

Dix, "Lice, rats, barbed wire, fleas . . ." is quoted in Jay Winter and Blaine Baggett, *The Great War and the Shaping of the Twentieth Century* (New York: Penguin Studio, 1996), pp. 99–101.

Freud, "the war in which we refused . . ." is from Freud, 1952, p. 756.

Freud, "tramples in a blind fury . . ." is from Freud, 1952, p. 757.

Freud, "the beauty of the snow-clad mountains . . ." is from Freud, 1952, p. 756.

Freud, "there is no such thing . . ." is from Freud, 1952, p. 758.

Sachs, "our overcoats and gloves . . ." is from Sachs, p. 154.

Freud, "I do not doubt that mankind . . ." is from Ernst Pfeiffer, ed., *Sigmund Freud and Lou Andreas-Salomé: Letters* (London: Hogarth Press and the Institute of Psycho-Analysis, 1972), p. 21.

Freud, "Such a choice of profession . . ." is from Sigmund Freud, *Introductory Lectures on Psychoanalysis,* in *The Standard Edition* . . . (vol. XV, 1961), p. 16.

Freud, "No meat, not enough bread . . ." is quoted in Clark, p. 395.

Freud, "We have grown hungry beggars . . ." is quoted in Gay, p. 381.

Freud, "I can't remember a time . . ." is quoted in Clark, p. 400.

Freud, "It is a senseless brutal act . . ." is quoted in Clark, p. 401.

Freud, "*The goal of all life is death . . .*" is from Freud, 1952, p. 652.

Freud, "The ego represents what we call reason . . ." is from Freud, 1952, p. 702.

Putnam, "Who would have dreamed . . ." is from James Putnam, "The Work of Sigmund Freud," *Journal of Abnormal Psychology*, August 1917, p. 146.

Mitchell, "Today, aided by German perplexities . . ." is quoted in Clark, p. 370.

CHAPTER NINE
ABANDONING SHIP

Anna Freud (daughter), "Papa wanted to show me . . ." is quoted in Elisabeth Young-Bruehl, *Anna Freud: A Biography* (New York: Summit Books, 1988), p. 120.

Freud, "I realize . . . for the first time . . ." is from Pfeiffer, p. 126.

Freud, "the Monster" is quoted in Clark, p. 446.

Freud, "It is no use quarreling . . ." is quoted in Jones, 1961, p. 475.

Freud, "Complete agreement . . ." is quoted in Jessie Taft, *Otto Rank: A Biographical Study Based on Notebooks, Letters, Collected Writings, Therapeutic Achievements and Personal Associations* (New York: Julian Press, 1958), p. 86.

Freud, "In my recent illness I learned . . ." is quoted in Lauzun, p. 104.

Freud, "At a time when no one in Europe . . ." is from Ernst L. Freud, p. 367.

Freud, "cheerful, sure of himself . . ." is quoted in Lauzun, p. 102.

Martin Freud, "When Jofi got up and yawned . . ." is from Martin Freud, p. 191.

Freud, "No pain, no grief . . ." is from Ernst L. Freud, p. 400.

Freud, "threatening calamities" is quoted in Lauzun, p. 104.

Freud, "What progress . . ." is quoted in Jones, 1961, p. 496.

Freud, "How a man of eighty feels . . ." is quoted in Jones, 1961, p. 507.

Freud, "Finis Austriae" is quoted in Martin Freud, p. 205.

CHAPTER TEN
"THE PATCHWORK OF LIFE'S LABOURS"

"His teachings have in their time . . ." is from an untitled notice in *The Lancet,* June 11, 1938, p. 1341.

Freud, "For the first time and late in life . . ." is from Ernst L. Freud, p. 448.

Anna Freud (daughter), "have been very friendly to us" is quoted in Berkley, p. 261n.

Freud, "You won't see me here . . ." is quoted in Hendrik M. Ruitenbeek, ed., *Freud As We Knew Him* (Detroit: Wayne State University Press, 1973), p. 313.

Freud, "Now it's nothing but torture . . ." is quoted in Max Schur, *Freud: Living and Dying* (New York: International Universities Press, 1972), p. 529.

Bernays, "America saw my brother's greatness . . ." is from Bernays, p. 342.

Brill, "Before he came on the scene . . ." is from "In Freud's Death World Loses a Pioneer in Science of Mind," *Science News Letter,* September 30, 1939, p. 221.

Overholser, "There is every reason to think . . ." is from "In Freud's Death World Loses a Pioneer in Science of Mind," p. 221.

"The microscope [revealed] the mystery . . ." is from Emanuel Miller, "The Significance of Freud." *The Nineteenth Century and After,* November 1939, p. 567.

Auden, "All he did was to remember . . ." is from W. H. Auden, "In Memory of Sigmund Freud," in Ruitenbeek, p. 117.

Freud, "I have in fact never done . . ." is quoted in Lauzun, p. 145n.

Jones, "How many of us, if we search . . ." is quoted in Lauzun, p. 145n.

Martha Freud, "How terribly difficult it is . . ." is quoted in Clark, p. 530.

Freud, "Looking back, then, over the patchwork . . ." is from Freud, 1963b, p. 134.

Berkley, George E. *Vienna and Its Jews: The Tragedy of Success, 1880s–1980s.* Lanham, Md.: Madison Books, 1988.

Clark, Ronald W. *Freud: The Man and the Cause.* New York: Random House, 1980.

Crankshaw, Edward. *The Habsburgs: Portrait of a Dynasty.* New York: Viking Press, 1971.

Freud, Ernst L., ed. *The Letters of Sigmund Freud.* New York: Basic Books, 1960.

Freud, Ernst, Lucie Freud, and Ilse Grumbrich-Simitis, eds. *Sigmund Freud: His Life in Pictures and Words.* New York: W. W. Norton, 1978.

Freud, Martin. *Sigmund Freud: Man and Father.* New York: Jason Aronson, 1983.

Freud, Sigmund. *An Autobiographical Study.* New York: W. W. Norton, 1963.

——. *Dora: An Analysis of a Case of Hysteria.* New York: Collier Books, 1963.

——. *The Major Works of Sigmund Freud.* William Benton, publisher. Chicago: Encyclopaedia Britannica, 1952.

——. *The Standard Edition of the Complete Psychological Works of Sigmund Freud.* 24 vols. James Strachey, general editor. London: Hogarth Press and the Institute of Psycho-Analysis, 1953–1974.

Gay, Peter. *Freud: A Life for Our Time.* New York: W. W. Norton, 1988.

Hunt, Morton. *The Story of Psychology.* New York: Doubleday, 1993.

Johnston, William M. *Vienna, Vienna: The Golden Age, 1815–1914.* New York: Clarkson N. Potter, 1980.

Jones, Ernest. *The Life and Work of Sigmund Freud.* New York: Basic Books, 1961.

Kramer, Peter D. *Listening to Prozac: A Psychiatrist Explores Antidepressant Drugs and the Remaking of the Self.* New York: Viking, 1993.

Maass, Walter B. *Country Without a Name: Austria Under Nazi Rule, 1938–1945.* New York: Frederick Ungar, 1979.

Miller, Jonathan, ed. *Freud: The Man, His World, His Influence.* Boston: Little, Brown, 1972.

Porter, Roy. *A Social History of Madness: The World Through the Eyes of the Insane.* New York: Weidenfeld and Nicholson, 1987.

Ruitenbeek, Hendrik M., ed. *Freud As We Knew Him.* Detroit: Wayne State University Press, 1973.

Segaller, Stephen, and Merrill Berger. *The Wisdom of the Dream: The World of C. G. Jung.* Boston: Shambhala, 1989.

Veith, Ilza. *Hysteria: The History of a Disease.* Northvale, N.J.: Jason Aronson, 1993.

Winter, Jay, and Blaine Baggett. *The Great War and the Shaping of the Twentieth Century.* New York: Penguin Studio, 1996.

Young-Bruehl, Elisabeth. *Anna Freud: A Biography.* New York: Summit Books, 1988.

GLOSSARY

analytic psychology: Psychoanalysis as revised by Carl Jung. Jung viewed the personal unconscious as a repository of intelligence and creativity. He also described the collective unconscious as the origin of the archetypes, those symbols and mythic figures that are meaningful in cultures throughout the world. The goal of Jungian analysis is to integrate the contents of the unconscious into a fully developed self.

catharsis: A release of pent-up emotions during psychotherapy that alleviates symptoms of distress.

complex: A set of interrelated emotions, impulses, and ideas that affects a person's behavior and mental state.

conversion: The unconscious process by which a repressed memory, emotion, or impulse gives rise to physical symptoms or illness.

defense mechanism: One of several unconscious processes that prevent painful or negative thoughts and impulses from entering consciousness or being acted upon directly.

denial: A common defense mechanism. A person in denial fails to see or acknowledge an unpleasant truth. Today we often recognize denial in persons with alcoholism or other addictions.

displacement: A defense mechanism in which an individual directs repressed feelings toward an acceptable substitute. For example, a person unable to admit anger at his or her parents might become enraged at politicians or other authority figures.

ego: The largely conscious part of the mind that represents reason and controls and directs the energy of the id.

Electra complex: A girl's desire for union with her father, combined with rivalry with her mother for the father's affection.

free association: The unguided, uncensored expression of ideas, memories, and impressions passing through the mind of a person undergoing analysis. Freud said that free association helps the analyst understand the patient's unconscious mental processes.

hysteria: In Freud's time, the term "hysteria" described a condition in which the patient displayed physical and emotional symptoms unrelated to any identifiable disease. While many doctors attributed hysteria to a disorder of the womb (uterus), Freud believed that it was psychological in origin.

id: The part of the mind that stores unconscious drives.

inferiority complex: Alfred Adler's term for the perceptions of psychological or physical inferiority that he believed account for neuroses. Adler saw parents who were too indulgent or too neglectful as the cause of the inferiority complex.

neurosis: A relatively mild mental or emotional disorder. Someone with a neurosis can distinguish reality from fantasy and is able to function in the world.

Oedipus complex: The desire in a child, especially a boy, for union with the parent of the opposite sex, and simultaneous feelings of rivalry with the parent of the same sex.

pleasure principle: The natural inclination to avoid pain and seek sensations that give pleasure.

projection: A common defense mechanism that allows an individual to attribute his or her own impulses to someone else.

psyche: A person's psychological structure; the mind.

psychoanalysis: The method developed by Freud for investigating unconscious mental processes and treating neuroses. The term "psychoanalysis" also refers to Freud's theories regarding conscious and unconscious mental activity.

psychosis: A severe mental disorder in which the individual's perception of reality is impaired.

rationalization: Someone employing this defense mechanism finds a worthy motive for behavior that really occurs for a less commendable reason.

reaction formation: A defense mechanism. A person exhibiting reaction formation displays or exaggerates a trait that is the opposite of one being repressed. For instance, the person may act especially loving toward someone he can't, even to himself, admit he hates.

repression: The process by which the conscious mind blocks out memories, emotions, or impulses that are too frightening or painful to acknowledge.

seduction theory: Freud's theory that all neuroses result from sexual abuse in childhood. Freud rejected the seduction theory in 1896.

sublimation: This is called the most positive defense mechanism. In sublimation, a person channels repressed energy into action that benefits society.

superego: The region of the mind that acts as the conscience. The superego contains the rules that the person has learned to live by; it determines right and wrong.

transference: The focusing of emotions, especially those experienced in childhood, onto someone other than the person who elicited the original feelings.

unconscious: The part of the mind that holds drives, memories, thoughts, and emotions of which the ego is unaware. The material in the unconscious can affect behavior.

INDEX

Note: Page numbers in **bold** type refer to illustrations.